DATE DUE			

33577000305423

**BIO
HALEY**

Gonzales, Doreen.

Alex Haley : author
of Roots

KANELAND HIGH SCHOOL LIBRARY

—PEOPLE TO KNOW—

Alex Haley

Author of *Roots*

Doreen Gonzales

Enslow Publishers, Inc.

40 Industrial Road	PO Box 38
Box 398	Aldershot
Berkeley Heights, NJ 07922	Hants GU12 6BP
USA	UK

http://www.enslow.com

Library of Congress Cataloging-in-Publication Data

Gonzales, Doreen.
    Alex Haley : author of Roots / Doreen Gonzales.
        p. cm. — (People to know)
    Includes bibliographical references and index.
    ISBN 0-89490-573-2
        1. Haley, Alex—Juvenile literature. 2. Historians—United
States—Biography—Juvenile literature. 3. Afro-American
historians—Juvenile literature. [1. Haley, Alex. 2. Authors,
American. 3. Afro-Americans—Biography.] I. Title. II Series.
E175.5.H27G66   1994
813'.54—dc20
[B]   93-44172
                                                                 CIP
                                                                  AC
Printed in the United States America

10 9 8 7 6 5 4 3

Illustration Credits:
Special thank you to George Haley for his permission to use photographs from the Alex P. Haley papers collection. Courtesy of the Special Collections Library, University of Tennessee, Knoxville, pp. 10, 13, 15, 19, 22, 24, 26, 30, 35, 55, 58, 63, 65, 76, 92, 100, 102, 115; Courtesy of the Special Collections at Hamilton College in Clinton, New York, p. 87. Courtesy of *Negro History Bulletin*, Vol. 40:2, Association for the Study of Afro-American Life and History, p. 80.

Cover Photo:
Special thank you to George Haley for his permission to use this photograph from the Alex P. Haley papers collection. Courtesy of the Special Collections Library, University of Tennessee, Knoxville.

Contents

1

Eighteen Cents and a Can of Sardines

Alex Haley did not know what to say. His friend had just offered him a job, and Alex could certainly use the money. Since 1959, Haley had been trying to earn a living as a writer. But during the last year he had sold only a few magazine articles. These sales had barely made Haley enough money to pay the rent on his one-room apartment. There had even been days when he didn't have money to buy food.

Now his friend was offering him a job with a good salary. If he took it he could buy a car and live in a nice apartment. He could even write in his free time. Finally Haley made up his mind.

"Thanks, but no," he told his friend. Unwilling to let go of his dream of becoming a writer, Alex Haley decided to stick it out a while longer.[1]

Later that day Haley had second thoughts. How could he turn down a good paying job when he was practically starving? He looked into the orange crate nailed to the wall that served as his kitchen cupboard. Inside were two cans of sardines and nothing else. The only money he had was the change in his pocket. He pulled it out—a dime, a nickel, and three pennies.

Feeling low, he thrust the coins into a paper sack. The sardines followed. "There, Alex," he said to himself. "There's everything you've made of yourself so far."[2]

As the days turned into weeks, and weeks into months, Haley was still collecting more rejections than acceptances for his writing. But he was also getting some work published. So he kept at it, and little by little, built a slow but steady record of sales.

Much of Haley's writing was about people he found interesting. And some of the most interesting people he knew were members of his own family.

Haley had been hearing stories about his family since childhood. He had spent many evenings in the little town of Henning, Tennessee, listening to his grandmother tell stories about their ancestors. Her stories reached all of the way back to his great-great-great-great-grandfather. This man, his grandmother had told him, was named Kin-tay and had been kidnapped in Africa by slave traders. Kin-tay had been brought to America and sold into slavery.[3]

These stories intrigued Haley. He knew that many of

his African-American friends didn't know much about their families' histories, partly because slave families were often separated when one member was sold to another plantation owner. Fortunately many of Haley's ancestors had been kept together as families. In addition they had kept their history alive in their memories. Each generation repeated over and over again their family history to the next generation, so the history would not be forgotten.[4]

Knowing about his ancestors made Haley feel part of a large family that extended back in time. He felt sorry for people who did not know anything about their ancestors.[5]

As he worked on different writing assignments, an idea began to take shape in his mind. What if he wrote a book about his family's history? No other African American had written about his or her ancestry. Perhaps it would help other African Americans feel connected to a past.[6]

Haley shared his idea with editors from the magazine *Reader's Digest.* They liked it and offered to help support him while he began to research his book.[7]

No one could have know then that it would be twelve years before Haley finished the book. As the years passed, he was often broke. He seemed to be constantly asking someone for money to continue his project.[8] But tedious hours of research often gave way to fascinating discoveries, and Haley maintained enthusiasm for his book.

When the research was complete, Haley labored at transforming hundreds of pages of notes into a book. Masterfully he wove his facts through a story that began with Kin-tay's life in Africa and ended with Haley himself. A short version of the book was printed in *Reader's Digest* in May 1974.

In October 1976 the book was finally published. Entitled *Roots: The Saga of an American Family*, it was an immediate success! Various critics called it brilliant, powerful, and eloquent. In a book review for the *Wall Street Journal*, Edmund Fuller wrote that *Roots* showed how the histories of black people and white people in America were linked together.[9] *The Final Days*, a book about President Nixon's last days in the White House was the best-selling nonfiction book in 1976. *Roots* came in second, even though it had only been available for three months.[10]

As Americans read *Roots*, television producers were busy making a twelve-hour movie version of the book. Haley moved to Los Angeles to help.

One hundred thirty million people watched at least one segment of the eight-night movie, which began on January 23, 1977. Sociologists, professors, and social activists across the country felt the miniseries improved race relations in America. *Time* magazine reported that "the gulf between black and white has been narrowed a bit and the level of mutual understanding has been raised a notch."[11]

Meanwhile, the book was creating its own sensation. On April 18, 1977 Alex Haley was awarded one of the most distinguished awards in American literature for *Roots*. He received the Pulitzer Prize because of the book's "important contribution to the literature of slavery."[12]

After more than thirty years of writing, Alex Haley had catapulted to success. *Roots* had made his dream come true—he was finally earning a comfortable living as an author.

Fame and wealth were new experiences for Haley. One day, while unpacking boxes in his Los Angeles home, he came across a brown paper sack. Inside he found two cans of sardines, a dime, a nickel, and three pennies.

Suddenly Haley remembered stuffing those items into the bag so many years earlier. Then, he said, "the past came flooding in like a riptide. I could picture myself once again huddled over the typewriter in that cold, bleak, one-room apartment. And I said to myself, 'The things in this bag are part of my roots, too. I can't ever forget that.' "[13]

Haley's long struggle to success suddenly had meaning. The poverty, the hard work, and the disappointments had all taught him something: dreams don't come easily. He had learned dreams take sacrifice,

Alex Haley had been writing for over a quarter of a century before his book, *Roots,* made him famous.

dedication, and determination to make them come true. Haley had the sardines and coins encased in clear plastic and hung this new trophy on the wall above his desk. Next to it were his Pulitzer Prize and a picture of several Emmy Awards the movie version of *Roots* had won.[14]

To people unfamiliar with Haley's story, the plastic plaque may have looked odd next to his other, more prestigious awards. But Haley knew the sardines and coins belonged with the awards. To him they represented the courage he had to keep working toward his goal. He worked even when the odds were against him—like on the day he turned down a job offer with eighteen cents to his name. If Haley had taken the job, who knows if he might have ever written *Roots*.

Upon reflection Alex Haley saw how many incidents and circumstances in his life had led him toward the writing of *Roots*. Though each one seemed meaningless by itself, when viewed together, the incidents became significant. Clearly they had led him, step-by-step, down the path to success.[15]

Looking back it was easy to see how various circumstances worked together to shape Haley's future. But while his life unfolded, no one could foresee how individual events would play a part in Alex Haley's destiny.

The Professor's Son

Lane College in Jackson, Tennessee, was where Simon Haley met Bertha Palmer. Both earned high school diplomas there—a rare distinction for any African American during the early 1900s. The two became engaged, and then Simon went on to college.

A college education was quite an accomplishment for the son of a sharecropper, but Simon had hungered for an education all his life. He was the first African American male in Savannah, Tennessee, to graduate from eighth grade. Afterward he moved to Jackson, where he took high school classes at Lane College. Because Simon's family was poor, he earned his own living expenses while going to school. Working and studying was exhausting, and many times Simon fell asleep with a book in his hands.

Simon Haley was the first member of his family to graduate from high school and then college. He hoped that someday his children would do something to make the world a better place.

Still, Simon graduated from high school, and in 1914, he enrolled in A & T University in Greensboro, North Carolina. Again he struggled to make money and keep up with his schoolwork.

The summer before his senior year, Simon worked as a porter on a train. As the months passed, he waited on passengers and saved as much money as he could. One night he served milk to a man who chatted with Simon about his schooling. At the time Simon thought little of their conversation.

By summer's end Simon had saved enough money to pay for one semester of school. He returned to college hoping to improve his grades now that all of his time could be devoted to studying.

Simon arrived on campus to surprising news. A Mr. Boyce had already paid his expenses! In a letter to the college president, Mr. Boyce identified himself as the man Simon had served milk.[1]

Simon earned his bachelor's degree that year, finishing first in his class. This distinction won him a scholarship for graduate studies at Cornell College in Ithaca, New York. But World War I temporarily interrupted his education. Simon entered military service in 1918. When he returned he headed for Henning, Tennessee, to marry his sweetheart Bertha Palmer.

In June 1920 the newlyweds boarded the Henning train bound for Ithaca, New York, where Simon would attend Cornell University.

Bertha Palmer Haley was an accomplished pianist. She died when Alex was ten years old.

At Cornell, Simon began course work in agriculture, working toward his master's degree. Meanwhile Bertha took piano lessons at the Ithaca Conservatory of Music. Her schooling, though, stopped in June 1921. Something else would soon be commanding her attention.

On August 11, 1921, Bertha gave birth to Alexander Murray Palmer Haley. Though the world would know him as Alex Haley, family and friends called him Palmer.

When Alex was six weeks old, the Haleys traveled back to Henning. Bertha and Alex would stay there while Simon returned to Cornell to continue his studies.

Bertha's father, Will Palmer, was no stranger to the ambition that Simon possessed. As a young man, Palmer had been ambitious too.

At age sixteen he went to work at the Henning Lumber Company, where the owner often neglected his business. Palmer corrected the owner's oversights whenever possible. When the man's business went bankrupt, Henning's white businessmen offered Palmer a loan on the company. He accepted, and in 1893, became the first black man in Henning to own a business.[2]

That same year Palmer married a young woman from Henning, Cynthia Murray. In 1895 their daughter, Bertha, was born.

Palmer was not only hard-working, he was charitable. He often donated money to his church,

16

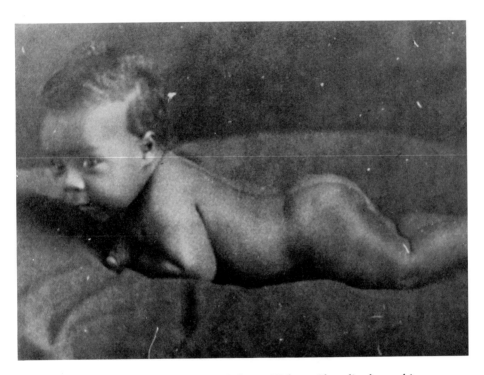

Infant Alexander Murray Palmer Haley, Alex lived at his grandparents' home in Henning, Tennessee, until he was a year old.

school, and community. He was generous to his daughter too.

At age eight Bertha was given a piano. At fifteen she received a Sears charge account to use as she wished. Sometimes Cynthia complained that Palmer was spoiling his daughter.

Still, when she left for Lane College, Palmer presented Bertha with her personal membership to the National Association for the Advancement of Colored People (NAACP). Simon and Bertha's wedding in 1920 was a huge affair—the town's first interracial social event. Perhaps Cynthia Palmer was right, her daughter was a bit indulged. But Bertha was an only child, and Palmer loved her very much.

When Bertha moved home with Alex in 1921, Will Palmer was beside himself with happiness. He doted on his new grandson and spent most of his free time with Alex. This ended when Simon took a teaching job at Lane College in 1922, and Bertha and Alex moved with him to Jackson.

During 1925, Bertha and Alex moved back to the Palmer house in Henning. Again Alex and his grandfather were the best of friends. Palmer took him everywhere—even to his office, where Alex played in his grandpa's big swiveling oak chair.

According to family stories, Haley began school when he was three years old. He went to the elementary school in Henning, where his mother helped teach. This

Alex's grandfather Will Palmer was an ambitious and charitable man.

was a special school that only African-American children attended. Schools were segregated then, blacks were not allowed in the same schools as whites.

For Alex's fourth birthday, his parents and grandparents gave him an unusual gift—a slice of a redwood tree. His father explained how each tree ring marked one year of growth. Then Simon pointed out the fifteen labels on the tree. Every one, he said, represented an important event that occurred during that particular year.

Among the events marked were the Emancipation Proclamation, the Civil War, and the birth of Alex's great-great-grandfather. Then Simon told Alex he could add his own labels to the tree.

The challenge to find events worthy of marking launched Alex into a childhood of voracious reading. "From then on, I read every book I could handle, along with my grandpa's newspapers for Black people," Alex later said.[3] Later that month Alex's brother George was born.

When Alex was four years old, Will Palmer died. Alex was hysterical over his death and remembers being given some sort of medicine to calm down.

Simon took over the lumber company for about a year. After putting Palmer's business affairs in order, Simon sold the company. He then took a teaching job at a college for African Americans in Langston, Oklahoma. The family moved to Langston, where Alex attended a grade school on the campus of the college.[4] As in Henning, the school was only for African Americans.

Simon returned to Cornell for further schooling in 1930. And in December of that year a third son was born. The Haleys named him Julius.

Upon receiving his master's degree in 1931, Simon was hired to teach agriculture at A. & M. College in Normal, Alabama. There, Alex and George attended the grade school on campus for African-American children. That year was a hard one for Bertha as she was suffering from tuberculosis.

One morning in February 1932, Alex and George received a message at school to hurry home. Knowing their mother had been sick, the boys ran the whole way—arriving at their mother's bed out of breath. They stood beside her for a few moments, and then she died. Bertha was taken to Henning to be buried.

For a short while Simon's mother Queen came to live with Alex's family in Normal. Then in 1933 Simon Haley married Zeona Hatcher, another professor on campus. The couple soon added a daughter, Lois, to their family.

While Zeona took care of the children, Simon continued his work as the head of the college's agriculture department. Simon was a dedicated educator who believed he could improve the conditions of African-American people by teaching them modern farming techniques. He often developed close

Simon, Bertha, and Alex outside the Palmer home in Henning.

relationships with his students, even letting a few live in his home.

Simon wanted his own children to get a good education too. He often stressed the importance of education, hoping his children could one day "improve the circumstances or the public perceptions of [the black] race."[5]

As a child, Alex heard over and over again about African Americans whose brilliance or courage had advanced the lives of other African Americans. Once Simon even took his sons to Tuskegee University to meet the famous African-American scientist, George Washington Carver.

But Alex was not the ambitious student his father had been. Usually he passed his school days dreaming. He loved nothing better than to sit by the window and watch the clouds float by.

Clearly Alex's favorite place was not school. Instead he seemed happiest at his grandmother's home in Henning, Tennessee. He and his brothers stayed there each summer, and Alex would grow up calling the Palmer house home.

The Palmer house was probably the grandest of any African-American home in Henning in the early 1900s. The two-story, ten-room home had a music parlor and a library. Books by outstanding people such as W.E.B. Dubois, Booker T. Washington, and Paul Lawrence Dunbar were ever available to Alex and his brothers.

Alex, about eight years of age, poses with his toy gun and younger brother George.

Summers also brought Alex back to his Henning pals. Two of them, Fred Montgomery and George Sims, would become Alex's lifelong friends.

As an adult, Montgomery remembered how Alex loved to dream. "Sometimes," Montgomery said, "in the middle of play, Alex would stop and look off in the distance, caught in a daydream."[6]

Montgomery also remembered how Alex saved his pennies and hid them on a ledge inside the Palmer house. Occasionally he would take one to buy himself some candy. But Alex might not keep the candy for long. If another youngster came by and asked Alex for it, he would give away his treat without hesitation.

In addition to the Haley boys, one or more of Alex's great aunts often visited the Palmer home in the summer. Each evening, when the supper dishes were done, the women sat on the porch and talked. Alex liked to sit behind his grandmother's rocking chair and listen to their stories.

Frequently the women talked about their family's ancestry, reciting and discussing the Murray genealogical line. The Murrays were proud of their ancestors, and they loved to retell tales of times gone by.

Mingled among the Murray ancestral stories were Bible stories and stories about other relatives such as Will Palmer and Simon Haley. Sometimes the stories and characters got all mixed up in Alex's head, and he confused the Bible stories with narratives of his family.

Alex gives George a lift. This photograph was taken while the Haleys were living on the campus of Langston College.

Other times, because he was a child, he had difficulty understanding just what the women were talking about.

One thing Alex did understand was that his family's history was important. As an adult, he realized that much of his self-esteem and personal identity had come from knowing that he had a long line of ancestors. The stories taught Alex other things too. Many emphasized determination and drive, and several stressed generosity. These were values Alex would live by all his life.

In high school, Alex took mathematics, English, history, and geography. In addition and at his father's insistence he took typing. But Alex still wasn't an exceptional student. He graduated from the A. & M. College high school in 1936 with a "C" average.[7]

Alex then enrolled in Alcorn A. & M. College in Lorman, Mississippi, where his father had taken a teaching job. When Simon moved from Alcorn to Elizabeth City Teacher's College in North Carolina, Alex transferred too.

As an adult, Alex's brother Julius could still remember the big white house the family lived in at the college. Julius fondly recalled how his whole family was together there. Though Alex never spoke of it publicly, Julius recalled times when Zeona taught at one school and Simon at another. During these periods the family would be broken apart. In Elizabeth City everyone was together. That didn't last long though.

Alex knew his father's "greatest dream was that his

three sons would become Ph.Ds."[8] But just as Simon Haley had yearned for an education, Alex yearned for something else. Exactly what it was, he didn't know. He did know that it wasn't more years at college. By June 1939 Alex had decided to drop out of school. "For a long time," Alex later said, "Dad didn't forgive me for that."[9]

The Coast Guard
School of Writing

Simon Haley decided that a three-year enlistment in the United States Coast Guard was what his son needed. He hoped Alex would come out of the service ready to pursue his education.

So Haley enlisted in the Coast Guard in the summer of 1939. Being African American he was automatically made a steward, the lowest rank possible. His duties ranged from cleaning officers' rooms to shining shoes. "There was only one way for a black to go in those days," Haley later remembered. "That system was unfair, very unfair, as I look back on it now, but I didn't see it as unfair then because that was the way things were outside at the time."[1]

Sometimes Haley's ship docked at a North Carolina

Because he didn't want to return to college, Haley joined the United States Coast Guard in 1939. This photograph was taken shortly after his enlistment.

port. It was here that he met his wife-to-be, Nan Branch. Haley and Branch were married in 1941.

Haley re-enlisted in 1942 and was assigned to the Elizabeth City Air Base. In 1943 he was transferred to the U.S.S. *Murzim*, a ship that carried ammunition for World War II.

The U.S.S. *Murzim* was often at sea for three months at a time. These long voyages were uneventful and monotonous. When the sailors finished their duties, they had to create their own amusements. Reading, Haley's childhood love, filled many of his free hours.

Haley also wrote letters. He wrote to his father, his teachers, his friends—just about anyone he could think of. It was not unusual for him to send out thirty or forty letters at a time. Haley came to think of his typewriter as his most precious possession on board ship.

Haley's supervisor, Scotty, saw his typing ability as an opportunity to catch up on his own letter writing. Each night Scotty would dictate letters as Haley typed. One night Scotty dictated a letter for a shipmate whose girlfriend had broken their engagement. Scotty was angry about her leaving his friend and told her she was cruel and uncaring. When the girl replied, begging forgiveness, the sailor was astonished.

Everyone on board soon heard about Scotty saving his friend's relationship. Believing that he must have a way with women, they asked him to write letters to their girlfriends. Scotty agreed and for several nights dictated love letters to Haley.[2]

Eventually Haley took over the composing of these letters. The sailors, jubilant with their girlfriends' responses, began paying Haley for his prose.

The pay made Haley wonder if he had a special talent for writing. One day he copied passages from a book, and for the first time, experienced "what good professional writing [felt] like."[3] This gave him the urge to see if he could do the same thing.

So Haley began writing love stories for magazines such as *Modern Romances* and *True Confessions.*

Though none were ever published, the experience helped an ambition to surface: Haley wanted to write. "The idea that one could roll a blank sheet of paper into a typewriter and write something on it that other people would care to read challenged, intrigued, exhilarated me."[4]

In 1945 the Coast Guard assigned Haley to an office in New York City. Haley lived in a neighborhood called Harlem. Harlem was an area with a large African-American population. The Haleys added to that population with their daughter Lydia, who was born in 1944, and son William, who came along in 1946.

At his job Haley manned the public information telephone and informed newspapers about incidents at sea. He took his job seriously and even had two telephone lines installed in his home. This way his wife could take information from the Coast Guard on one phone while Haley passed it to newspapers on the other.

In a few years Haley had earned the respect of many New York City newspaper reporters. In a tribute to Haley, the reporters wrote that he was "amiable, industrious and ever helpful. . . . If he's got it," they said, "you have it. If he hasn't got it, he'll get it—that's Haley."[5]

Haley's superiors noticed his diligence too. Soon he was the editor of a Coast Guard magazine called *The Helmsman*, had begun another magazine called *The Outpost*, and was a regular contributor to a third—*The United States Coast Guard Magazine*. When he wasn't working, Haley wrote articles of his own to sell. Each day he rose at 4:30 A.M. to write before leaving for work.

Now Haley was writing stories about the sea. Many of them were authentic adventures he found in old Navy files. But none of these sold either. Haley received one rejection after another. His writing was just not good enough—probably because he had little training in writing in high school or college.

However by reading, writing, and copying good writing, Haley was teaching himself to write. Unfortunately the benefits of his work were not immediate. Month after month, year after year, Haley received nothing but rejection letters. Each time a new one arrived, he pasted it to the wall. Before long his walls were covered with rejection slips.

But the rejections didn't destroy Haley's ambition. He knew they were a part of the writing profession. So he didn't give up. Still each time a magazine turned him down, he wondered if his writing was really good enough to sell.

Then one day in 1946, Haley received a letter that looked like the usual rejection—except for one thing. On it an editor had pencilled a simple, but inspiring note. "Nice try," it read.[6] Those two words kept Haley going.

In December 1949 Haley was promoted. Now he would be the Coast Guard's Chief Journalist, the first one the Coast Guard ever had. As such, Haley would write speeches for officers and stories for various publications.

Haley continued writing on his own too. In 1950 an editor finally bought one of his stories. Haley could hardly believe it! He had sold a story about the Coast Guard called "They Drive You Crazy" to *This Week* magazine.

Overjoyed by this small success, Haley continued sending out his stories. One day a writer named Glenn Klitter came into Haley's Coast Guard office to research an article. Klitter awed Haley. He admired Klitter's coat, and even wanted to touch it, marveling that it had been purchased with money earned from writing.[7]

Haley answered Klitter's questions, then told him about his own dream of becoming a writer. As they

During the 1950s, Haley worked as Chief Journalist for the Coast Guard. He and his staff reported Coast Guard news in various publications.

talked, Klitter mentioned that *Coronet* magazine was looking for the kind of dramatic narratives Haley was writing.

So Haley rushed four stories to *Coronet*. Three weeks later the *Coronet* editor called to say he was buying three of them. "The fourth one," the editor said, "is lousy."[8]

During the next three years Haley would write several more stories for *Coronet*. Many of these were published under a pen name. But Haley didn't care. The sales were evidence that he was mastering his chosen trade.

Haley had continued re-enlisting in the Coast Guard since entering in 1939. In 1954 he was transferred to San Francisco. Haley drove to California, stopping each night at a motel with a vacancy sign. But though they had vacant rooms, many motel clerks told Haley they had nothing available. Several nights he had nowhere to sleep but in his car.

Segregation and discrimination had always been a part of Haley's life. As a child he had not been allowed to attend the same public schools as white children. He had attended all-black colleges. And when he joined the Coast Guard, he was assigned the lowest rank, while white men with the same education were given a higher rank. Yet for some reason, these incidents had never bothered Haley.

But now, while traveling across the United States dressed in a military uniform decorated with medals, the discrimination made Haley angry. Years later he would describe this trip as the first time prejudice made him furious.[9]

Still, being African American was only a part of Haley's life. Being a writer was a much larger part, and it was becoming increasingly important.

By 1959 Haley had spent twenty years in the Coast Guard and was eligible for retirement. Ready for a change, he retired, his sights now set on becoming a full-time writer.

Haley and Malcolm X

From San Francisco, Haley set out for New York City, where he and his wife had decided to live separately. Haley's boyhood friend George Sims managed an apartment building there now, and Haley rented a room in the building's basement. It was cold and had no bathroom, but Haley didn't mind. What mattered was that he could spend all of his time writing.

Haley's new home was in a neighborhood of New York City called Greenwich Village. During the 1960s, Greenwich Village was filled with various artists who lived simple lives. Two of Haley's neighbors, artist Joe Delaney and singer Harry Belafonte became role models to Haley. They too were sacrificing material wealth to pursue their arts.

Now Haley's only income came from writing. His

Coast Guard retirement checks went to his wife who was raising their two children. For many months Haley wrote constantly and sold some of his work. But living only on the income from his writing sales was difficult. At times Haley wondered if he had made the right career choice. Did he truly have the talent to make it as a full-time writer?

Looking for support and guidance, Haley wrote to six African-American writers who also lived in Greenwich Village. Only one responded—James Baldwin. Baldwin was already a well-known author with two published books. During the 1960s he would gain more fame writing about racial conflict and civil rights.

When Baldwin appeared at Haley's door, the two men began a friendship that would last all their lives. At their first meeting, Baldwin treated Haley with respect, clearly regarding him as a fellow writer. Haley said later that this treatment did more for his confidence than Baldwin could ever know.[1]

Yet life was still precarious. When a friend from San Francisco called in 1960 to offer Haley a job, Alex was torn. Did he really want to continue this day-to-day existence, never knowing if he'd have enough money to buy food or pay the rent? After much soul searching, Haley decided that, yes, his dream was worth the struggle. Unless he stuck out the hard times, he would always wonder if he could be a writer.

Recently Haley had been hearing a lot about the

Nation of Islam, a religion based on the Islamic faith. Islam was and is the most popular religion in northern Africa and the Middle East. Today approximately nine hundred million people in the world practice Islam. They are known as Muslims.

Led by a man named Elijah Muhammad, the Nation of Islam was gaining popularity among African Americans. It combined traditional Islamic beliefs with the belief that black people were superior to white people. This group came to be known as the Black Muslims.

Haley suggested to the editors of *Reader's Digest* magazine that he write an article about the Nation of Islam. The editors liked the idea and gave Haley his first free-lance writing assignment.

At the time Haley had no way of knowing that this article would set events in motion that would affect the rest of his writing career. For now he was busy gathering information about the Nation of Islam from one of its chief spokesmen, a man named Malcolm X.

The Nation of Islam taught that both the United States and Christianity had failed African Americans. However, by becoming a devout Muslim and adhering to strict conduct rules, African Americans could rise above white people.

Persons who joined the Nation of Islam used the letter X as their last name. The X symbolized the African name that was lost when these persons' ancestors were enslaved. The Nation's message appealed to many African Americans who had faced racism and discrimination.

In his article Haley reported that one of every three hundred African Americans was a registered Black Muslim with "anti-white, anti-Christian, resentful, militant, [and] disciplined" beliefs.[2] Haley's first nationally published social commentary came at the end of the article. He wrote, "It is important for Christianity and democracy to help remove the Negroes' honest grievances and thus eliminate the appeal of such a potent racist cult."[3]

Editors at *Reader's Digest* liked Haley's article and published more of his work. In March 1961 he wrote about his Coast Guard boss Scotty. In May came a story about the African-American Olympic track champion Wilma Rudolph. Haley even wrote about his brother George, who had been the first African American to attend the University of Arkansas School of Law.

In the early 1960s universities and schools across the country were slowly integrating. But there were still many places where African Americans were not allowed. Black people commonly faced other kinds of discrimination too. During this time many African Americans joined together to fight for their rights.

Some African Americans belonged to the Southern Christian Leadership Conference, a group led by Dr.

Martin Luther King, Jr. King believed in fighting racial inequality through peaceful nonviolent protest.

Other African Americans believed they would have to use violence to secure equal rights. Members of the Nation of Islam held this belief. More and more Malcolm X was in the news speaking about his religious group's militant views.

Meanwhile *Playboy* magazine was beginning a new interview feature, and Haley was chosen to do the first one. He interviewed and wrote about musician Miles Davis. Readers liked the feature, and *Playboy* hired Haley to do another—this time of Malcolm X.

During this interview Malcolm said that "the white race, which is guilty of having oppressed and exploited and enslaved our people here in America, should and will be the victims of God's divine wrath."[4] Malcolm warned white Americans that soon they would "have to pay for the crime committed when their grandfathers made slaves out of us."[5]

Many Americans, both black and white, felt that this kind of talk was too extreme. They were afraid it would lead to riots and bloodshed. Haley agreed. In an article in the *New York Times Magazine*, he chastised militant leaders such as Malcolm X. Haley wrote:

> Privately not a few Negro leaders do wish that there was somewhat less demand for a regular fare of headline-making, "dramatic" statements and actions. These consume time that might be more

effectively spent in quiet, tough, statesmanlike bargaining, behind the scenes with local and national white power structures.[6]

Though Malcolm X's views were generally unpopular, the *Playboy* interview fascinated Ken McCormick from Doubleday and Company, a book publisher. McCormick believed that people would find a book about Malcolm's life equally fascinating. McCormick asked Malcolm if he would tell the details of his life in a full-length book. Malcolm said that he would consider doing such a book, but he was not a writer.

Then, Haley said, "because I had happened to be the black writer who had worked with Malcolm on most of the magazine articles about him or his organization, he asked me if I would be willing to work with him on this book. I was pleased and flattered to do so."[7]

Even so Malcolm worried that Haley would twist his words and ideas. He warned, "A writer is what I want, not an interpreter."[8] Haley promised that nothing would be put into the book that Malcolm didn't say. He also agreed that nothing would be left out that Malcolm wanted in.[9]

Three or four nights each week for about a year, Malcolm visited Haley's Greenwich Village apartment to talk. At first the men were somewhat uneasy with each other, and Malcolm seemed uncomfortable talking about his personal life. In fact Malcolm seldom talked about himself. Instead he spoke mostly about the Nation of Islam or Elijah Muhammad.

Haley was frustrated. His book was supposed to be about Malcolm X, not the Nation of Islam. Finally he asked Malcolm about his mother. That night Malcolm talked until dawn.

Soon Haley discovered another way to get information from Malcolm. During one session, Haley noticed Malcolm had scribbled notes on his coffee napkin. From then on, Haley always put napkins near Malcolm and gathered them when he left.

On one Malcolm wrote, "When I was released from prison, the first 3 items I purchased were: 1) eye glasses, 2) a watch, 3) a suitcase (so I could see what time it is and where to travel) and I've been on the move geographically (and upward) ever since."[10] Notes such as these helped Haley learn what Malcolm was thinking.

The interview sessions continued throughout 1964. As Malcolm told Haley about his life, Haley sat in a corner of his apartment and typed notes.

Sometimes Haley walked with Malcolm through Harlem and listened as he talked with the people on the street. On these strolls it was clear to Haley that Malcolm was a hero to the African Americans who lived there. As Malcolm moved down the sidewalks, Haley took notes in two different notebooks. In one he wrote information he wanted to include in the book. In the other notebook Haley wrote personal observances of Malcolm for his own use.

Malcolm introduced Haley to important African Americans during their months together, people such as author Louis Lomax and historian Dr. C. Eric Lincoln. Also, due to his writing, Haley met other prominent African Americans during this time. For example, he met Dr. Martin Luther King when he did a *Playboy* interview of him.

Haley was struck by the similarities between Malcolm X and King, even though they held such opposing viewpoints. Both he said, "were obsessed with their work but felt guilty about being away from their families."[11] And neither cared about acquiring any material possessions.

In 1964 Malcolm X left the Nation of Islam to adopt traditional Islam. Leaving the group that had meant so much to Malcolm was a difficult and tangled process. Many Muslims were angered by his departure.

But Malcolm was confident he wanted to belong to the Islamic faith worshipped in Africa. To learn more about it, he took two trips to Africa where he worshipped with Muslims of all colors. Their respect for each other changed his ideas. He now believed it was possible for people of all races to live together peacefully.

But Malcolm still believed that worldwide unity among blacks was important. So during his visits to

Africa, Malcolm met with African leaders, hoping to create a global organization for black people.

Haley recognized how Malcolm's travels in Africa deeply affected him, making him more accepting of others and at peace with himself. To Malcolm, the African journeys were his "ultimate spiritual homecoming, a return at last to the lost Eden."[12]

When Haley was ready to begin writing Malcolm's biography, he had already spent over 950 hours interviewing him. To write he retreated to Rome, New York, where George Sims and his parents were living. Haley had always thought of Sims' parents as substitute parents of his own.

In Rome, Haley lived in a building that had once been a small store. He taped newspapers over the windows so no one could see in. For sixteen to eighteen hours a day he worked on his book. Occasionally he would talk to Malcolm by phone or drive somewhere to meet him. From time to time Malcolm would remark that he would not live to see his autobiography published.

By February 1965 Haley had almost completed the book. On February 20, 1965, Malcolm phoned Haley and told him, "You know, I'm glad I've been the first to establish official ties between Afro-Americans and our blood brothers in Africa."[13]

On February 21, 1965, Malcolm X was assassinated. After Malcolm's death, Haley wrote an epilogue for his book. In it he described Malcolm as "the most electric personality I have ever met."[14]

Malcolm was killed at a time of turbulence within the Nation of Islam. Some Muslims, like Malcolm, had left the religion to join other groups. Others remained fiercely loyal to Elijah Muhammad and denounced those who left. They would most likely be angered by a book about Malcolm X.

Doubleday executives knew this and worried about their many bookstores around the nation named Doubleday. Would the Black Muslims retaliate with violence in these bookstores? Fearing injury to people or property, Doubleday and Haley agreed to sell *The Autobiography of Malcolm X* to Grove Press.

Doubleday sent the ready-to-print manuscript to Grove, and *The Autobiography of Malcolm X,* as told to Alex Haley, was published in the fall of 1965. Of it Haley said, "The book represents the best I could put on paper of what Malcolm said about his own life from his own mouth. I'm glad the book exists because otherwise Malcolm would be a pile of [ingenuine] and self-serving stories."[15]

When *The Autobiography of Malcolm X* was published, the public didn't know that four sections of the book were left out. The omitted chapters contained Malcolm's plan to help African Americans reach equal economic status with whites. No one has since explained why the chapters were not in the book. Some people believe that if Malcolm had been alive when the book was published, he would have enforced his original agreement with Haley and insisted the chapters be left in.

But even with sections missing, Haley's book was well received. Reviewers agreed that Haley had crafted the book well. Critic Truman Nelson said, "The reader must put aside any prejudice he may have about a book 'as told to' someone. You can hear and feel Malcolm in this book; it is a superb job of transcription."[16]

Haley's book soon became required reading for many college courses, and it was eventually selected as one of the ten best books of the 1960s. The book was popular with the general public too. It was not unusual to see young African Americans carrying around the book.

Most importantly, though, *The Autobiography of Malcolm X* was a book with a lasting message for people of all races and nations. It showed how poverty and racism work together to oppress people. In addition it demonstrated how people's life experiences determine how they view the world. One critic, I.F. Stone, said Haley's book was written with sensitivity and devotion. He predicted it would "have a permanent place in the literature of the Afro-American struggle."[17]

Malcolm's death made many people realize what a powerful leader he had been. Haley saw this too, and packed away a copy of the manuscript that contained

Malcolm's notes. Haley told a friend he was saving the copy because it might become "quite valuable, in time."[18]

Haley could have quit writing and lived comfortably on royalties from his first book. But he didn't. He had another idea.

The Evolution of an Idea

The last five years had been a time of change for Haley personally. After eighteen years of marriage he began living alone. Then in 1964 he and Nan Branch were divorced, and Haley married Juliette Collins. Subsequently they had a daughter Cynthia.

These years had brought change to Haley's writing career too. Not only had he published his first book, he had also published several articles in popular national magazines.

By 1965 four interviews by Haley had appeared in *Playboy* magazine, and he was developing a reputation as a fine interviewer. In the process Murray Fisher, the magazine's assistant editor, and Haley had become friends.

But it wasn't friendship that earned Haley the

writing assignments. It was his ability to get insightful interviews from newsworthy personalities. For instance Malcolm X, who had refused to speak to white journalists, talked to Haley.

On the other hand George Lincoln Rockwell, leader of the American Nazi Party, didn't want to be interviewed by a black person. When Haley told him he had a white ancestor and insisted it would be his "white part" interviewing Rockwell, the Nazi leader gave in. Rockwell later said that Haley had "charmed his storm troopers."[1]

From movie stars to the leaders of social reform, Haley could get a good interview from almost anyone. He thoroughly prepared for his interviews, studying his subject until he was genuinely interested in the person. During the interview Haley took his time and asked sincere questions.

When he wasn't getting new information from a subject, Haley relied on the trick he had learned writing about Malcolm X—he asked the person about his or her childhood.

Writing Malcolm X's biography had taught Haley other skills too. For example he had learned how to make readers feel compassion for someone as unpopular as Malcolm X. Haley had begun the book with Malcolm's birth and childhood. He knew readers would sympathize with a child growing up so poor he was dizzy with hunger. Once the reader cared about young

Malcolm, Haley reasoned, the reader would care about the adult Malcolm. This emotional bond made Malcolm's radical ideas easier to understand.

Not only had critics and scholars applauded Haley's first book, his father had praised him too. Simon Haley now wrote to his son, "I think I will consider [publishing a book] equivalent to your degree."[2]

Though his writing had kept him busy, Haley had taken time to encourage other writers. One, Ann Crawford, met Haley when she was just beginning her career. Haley had inspired and convinced her to keep writing. "Without Alex Haley's words of encouragement," Crawford later wrote, "I may not have even tried."[3]

Helping others succeed was a Haley family tradition. In his childhood Haley had heard many stories about relatives helping others up the ladder of success. Now, as a published author, Haley felt obligated and honored to share his knowledge.

Other childhood stories had stuck with Haley too. During the past five years he had been thinking about the ancestral stories he had heard years before on his grandmother's porch in Henning, Tennessee.

Now over forty years old Haley could easily distinguish the Bible stories from the stories of his ancestors. He also understood more about how American society functioned during the various time periods that the stories took place.

But Haley's story collection was like a patchwork quilt with several squares missing. The bits he did know were scattered among different branches of his family and throughout two centuries. Some stories were from his mother's side of the family and some were from his father's. Some tales went back several generations while others were about his own parents. To Haley these stories had a charm and drama all their own.

As Haley was finishing the *Malcolm X* book, he wrote to Doubleday editors, proposing he write a book about his mother's maternal ancestors. The book would tell how the Murrays settled in Tennessee after the Civil War. Because Haley planned to show how his relatives lived peacefully with whites, he decided to call his book, *Before This Anger*. The Doubleday editors liked the idea, and in 1964, hired Haley to write such a book.

Haley was now putting the finishing touches on *The Autobiography of Malcolm X*. In it Haley had written:

> Human history's greatest crime was the traffic in black flesh when the devil white man went into Africa and murdered and kidnapped . . . millions of black men, women, and children who were worked and beaten and tortured as slaves. The devil white man cut these black people off from all knowledge of their own kind, and cut them off from any knowledge of their own language, religion, and past culture, until the black man in America was the earth's only race of people who had absolutely no knowledge of his true identity.[4]

Haley remembered a story his grandmother had told that illustrated Malcolm's point. The story was about the family's African ancestor who had been kidnapped from his homeland and thrust into slavery in America. With no regard for his personal history or identity, his American captors replaced the African's name with an American name, Toby. According to the story, the African strongly objected to his new name and insisted he was Kin-tay, not Toby.

Over the years Haley had heard other African Americans speak about their lost African heritage. In Haley's interview of King, for example, King had told him, "[The American Negro] feels a deepening sense of identification with his black African brothers. . . . We are descendents of the Africans. Our heritage is Africa."[5]

In fact African Americans across America seemed to be thinking about their roots. Haley too wondered about his history. Who were the ancestors he didn't know? Where had they lived? What had their lives been like?

In 1964 Haley visited the National Archives in Washington, D.C., looking for documents that might mention his ancestors. Remembering that his grandmother's family had lived in Alamance County, North Carolina, Haley found a census of that county taken in the year 1870. In the census, he came across the names of his grandmother's parents and siblings.

Seeing his relatives' names in official documents struck Haley as hugely significant. To him it proved that

While researching *Before This Anger*, Haley found a census record that listed his great-grandparents Tom and Irene Murray. They were the parents of Haley's grandmother Cynthia Murray Palmer.

he, his family—and indeed—all black people, "did have a past, a heritage."[6]

Haley had planned to plunge into the writing of *Before This Anger* as soon as he completed *Malcolm X*. But now he couldn't. His interest in his personal history drove him to learn more.

So Haley visited the National Archives and Library of Congress as often as he could, looking for wills, deeds, or any other records that might yield information about his ancestry. While he searched, America continued to struggle with race relations. African Americans were becoming more dissatisfied, and their leaders more vocal.

Haley's friend James Baldwin said, " . . . from where I sit, and from where my brothers are huddling tonight in their black ghettos from Boston to San Diego, we can't wait for laws that take so long to pass and then so much longer—it seems forever—to enforce. We're ready now. We've been ready for generations."[7]

Haley himself had spoken with many African-American leaders. He had heard them propose a variety of solutions to racial strife—from total segregation to complete integration. Though various leaders offered different solutions, all of them were concerned about restoring rights and dignity to African Americans.

Haley was neither a politician nor a social activist. He was a writer. In some way he wanted to use his writing to improve the African-American condition.

Civil rights, African brothers, lost heritage—these ideas swirled around one part of Haley's mind, while questions about unknown ancestors swirled around another part. Gradually the separate concepts converged, creating one new idea.

Could *Before This Anger* be transformed into a book about African-American ancestry? Specifically, could Haley locate the missing pieces of his own genealogical line and follow them in story from slavery to his generation?

Haley knew researching such a book would be difficult. There had been very few written records kept of African Americans. Yet the thought was too exciting to let go. Haley told one interviewer, "It's going to be a big book, take a lot of work, but imagine—from an African slave to [a writer!]"[8]

To help him research his past, Haley recruited George Sims. The two quickly became absorbed in their quest. A friend recalls walking into Haley's apartment one day to find Haley and Sims engaged in serious conversation. "They had all these little slips of paper on a big table in front of them," he said, and they went on talking, not even noticing he was there.[9]

In 1966 Haley wrote to *Reader's Digest*, describing his idea. Impressed with the concept the editors pledged to help Haley financially. Each month for a year he would receive three hundred dollars, plus necessary travel expenses.[10]

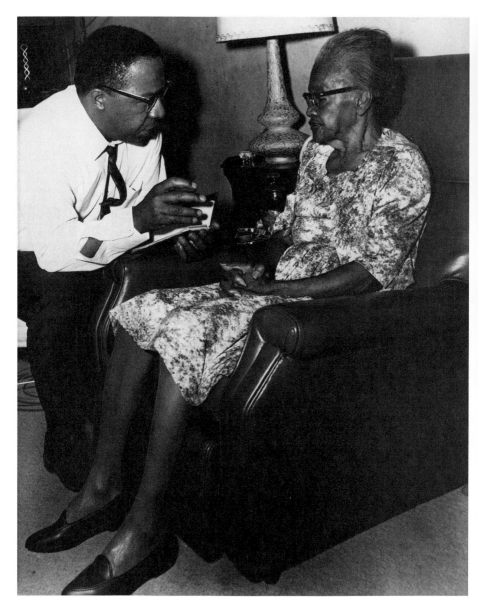

To learn more about the old family stories, Haley traveled to Kansas City to gather information from his "Cousin Georgia." She was the sole surviving storyteller from Haley's youth.

That fall Haley spoke at Hamilton College in Clinton, New York. Most of his presentation was about *The Autobiography of Malcolm X*. But he also hinted about the new book he was researching. This book, he said, would "tell the story of his slave ancestors."[11]

After his lecture Haley visited Hamilton frequently to participate in group discussion programs. One professor at the college was so impressed by Haley that he convinced the college president to hire Haley as a writer-in-residence. In exchange for a home on campus, Haley instructed a class. "[I wasn't] really a teacher," Haley later said, "but like Grandma, I talked about things that interested me."[12]

Those subjects apparently interested others too. Professor Todd reported that students were so thrilled by Haley's stories, they hated missing class. Later Haley was praised for teaching what came to be known as "a course in Alex Haley."[13]

Haley seemed to have a talent for enthralling people. One night at a dinner party Haley spent the evening fascinating the guests with stories about his ancestors.

When another group invited Haley to their gathering, some members were upset because Haley was African American. They decided they would not attend. When they were finally persuaded to come, they were the people with the highest praise for Haley after he spoke!

Early in Haley's association with Hamilton College,

he met Ebou Manga, a student from The Gambia, Africa.[14] Soon after their introduction, Haley asked Manga if he could translate some African words that had been passed down with the family stories about Kin-tay the slave. Manga recognized the words as Mandinkan, the language of the Mandingo people from The Gambia.[15]

The discovery gripped Haley. Was Kin-tay from The Gambia? Was there a way to trace him to his African home? To Haley the possibility was fascinating, and he knew there was only one way to find the answer.

He was going to Africa!

Africa!

By 1967 Haley felt he had identified his maternal ancestors seven generations back to the African whom he believed arrived in America in 1767. With Ebou Manga's help, Haley hoped to trace Kin-tay to his African home.

But hundreds of thousands of Africans had come to North America in chains, and none was ever identified by name. Finding the origin of one black man among thousands seemed impossible.

Haley held out one hope: Manga had told him about African men called griots. Griots were trained since childhood to memorize histories of various families. Many could recite particular family trees going back many generations.

The very existence of griots amazed and intrigued

Haley. "It astounds [me] now to realize that men like these, in not only Africa but other cultures, can literally talk for days, telling a story and not repeating themselves."[1]

When Manga and Haley flew to The Gambia in the spring of 1967, Haley met with a group of Gambian tribal leaders. They told him that Kin-tay (properly spelled Kinte) was a common Gambian name, and they promised to look for a griot who knew the Kinte lineage.

In six weeks Haley returned to The Gambia. The leaders had found an old man in the village of Juffure who might be able to help. In Juffure, Haley was introduced to Kebba Kanji Fofana. Fofana answered Haley's questions and told him about a young man named Kunta Kinte who had disappeared from Juffure in the 1760s.

Haley later described the moment when he realized Fofana's Kunta Kinte must be his Kin-tay:

> I sat as if I were carved of stone. My blood seemed to have congealed. This man whose lifetime had been in this back-country African village had no way in the world to know that he had just echoed what I had heard all through my boyhood years on my grandma's front porch in Henning, Tennessee . . . of an African who always had insisted that his name was "Kin-tay" . . . and who had been kidnaped into slavery while not far from his village.[2]

Haley seemed to have accomplished what no other

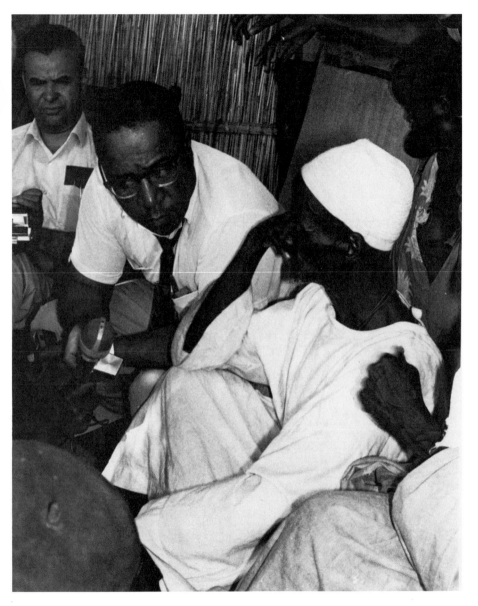

Haley speaks with Kebba Kanji Fofana during his second trip to
Africa. Haley's friend and researcher George Sims listens in the
background.

American had done. He had traced his ancestry from twentieth-century America to an eighteenth-century African village.

It occurred to Haley that because every African American goes back ancestrally to someone who lived in Africa, any one of them with enough clues could trace his or her roots to Africa through a griot.

Unfortunately slave families were frequently separated and children often grew up not knowing who their parents were. Few African Americans, therefore, had any clues about their pre-Civil War ancestry.

But Haley's family was unique. Many of his predecessors had kept their families together one way or another. And the family's oral history had been passed down through the generations.

Just as Haley's original idea for *Before This Anger* had grown before, his concept broadened again. His book, he decided, would begin in Africa, describing Kinte's childhood, capture, and enslavement. He would then follow Kinte's descendents to himself.

But Haley's book would be more than the story of his African-American family. Symbolically it would belong to all African Americans. It would represent the ancestry of every one of them, "for all of us today to know who we are."[3] Haley hoped his book would restore identity and pride to African Americans.

When Haley returned from The Gambia, he began work on his book. The quiet Hamilton campus was the

Haley poses in Juffure with Fofana and African members of the
Kinte family.

perfect place to contemplate his new plans. He appreciated taking long peaceful walks around campus, and being near students and professors with whom he could discuss his writing.

To Haley, it seemed that this new book would be popular to African Americans. When he occasionally ran into Professor Todd on campus, he would tell him, "Man, I've got a bear by the tail—it's just the biggest thing that ever happened to me!"[4] And he wrote a letter to James Baldwin, saying, "I have a big one, baby."[5]

By the end of 1967 Haley was hard at work shaping his book. According to Professor Todd, "The lights in his little hideaway often burned all night; George Sims spent more and more time with him, and notes appeared frequently on his class blackboard announcing 'Mr. Haley will not hold classes this week.' "[6]

Just as he had aroused sympathy for Malcolm X, Haley planned to do the same with Kinte. His story would begin with Kinte's birth and follow him as he grew toward manhood, describing the customs and religious rites Kinte would experience. This, Haley hoped, would make Kinte's capture and enslavement most wrenching.

Haley realized that to make his book authentic, there were many topics about which he needed to know more. He left Hamilton College in 1969 to continue his research.

First Haley needed to learn more about

eighteenth-century African culture. So he visited The Gambia several times, traveling to the backcountry to talk with Mandinkan elders. They told Haley about their ways, often relating anecdotes of their own childhoods to him.

Haley was particularly charmed by the way Mandinkan babies were named. The father of a newborn stopped all activity for seven days and did nothing but think of a name for the child. On the eighth day the father whispered the name to the infant before telling anyone else. The Africans believed a child should be the first to know who he or she was. Haley found it ironic that African Americans knew so little about themselves, but the Africans from whom they descended seemed to know so much.

In addition Haley traveled to England to study the records of early missionaries in Africa. While there he also researched the slave trade, learning of the wretched conditions under which Africans were transported to America.

During this research Haley came across a slave ship captain named John Newton. Newton was almost killed in a shipwreck. This near-death experience awakened him to the immorality of slavery. So Newton became a minister and preached against slavery. He also authored several hymns, including the popular "Amazing Grace."

For another part of his book, Haley researched American slavery by studying the diaries and letters of southerners before the Civil War. Most helpful, though, were the testimonies of ex-slaves themselves. He read these in a book called *Lay My Burden Down*.

It would take Haley four years to collect all of the information he needed. Throughout this period, his finances were always a problem. Doubleday and *Reader's Digest* continued to give him periodic advances, but this money never lasted long enough.

So Haley supplemented his income by lecturing about his forthcoming book. When he ran out of advance money, he stopped writing to lecture. Then when he saved enough to return to writing, he quit lecturing.

Though not a trained speaker, Haley had a voice Murray Fisher once described as a "deep, down-home baritone he can pour on like honey over biscuits."[7] This trait, plus Haley's personal enthusiasm, impressed and excited audiences. When he spoke at Northwestern University in Illinois in 1968, student James Turner described Haley as a spellbinding storyteller with a riveting story.

Storytelling was a familiar form of entertainment to Haley. Each generation of his family, Haley said, had produced a storyteller. He supposed he was his generation's.

But even with lecturing, Haley's bills mounted. At times he was so broke he had to borrow from his friends. "I owed everybody I had been able to borrow from,"

Haley said. "It was humiliating."[8] At one point Haley estimated that between individuals and various lending institutions, he owed a total of $100,000.

Haley had other troubles too. He and Juliette were divorced in 1972. He believed this marriage, like the last, had failed because of his writing. "In both cases," he said, "the 'other woman' was a typewriter."[9]

In addition, for much of his adulthood, he had not been a very good father. He had been so occupied with his writing, he had made little time for his children.

Finally, after four years of research, Haley knew it was time to begin writing. But he wasn't sure he could complete the task he had set out for himself. He was overwhelmed with the abundance of material he had amassed and wondered how he could ever organize it into a book.

Haley had already missed five deadlines his publishers had set. Doubleday was waiting for his book, *Reader's Digest* was waiting for it, his creditors, his friends—everyone, it seemed to Haley, was waiting for him to write the book he had promised for so long.

One night, while returning from Africa by ship, Haley reflected on his situation in despair. Walking on deck, he looked into the ocean and considered suicide. "All I'd have to have done was step between the rails," Haley said.[10]

Fortunately something called him back. Haley said

he heard his ancestors' voices talking to him. They were urging him on, telling him not to give up.

His personal mission also called him back. Haley felt a grave responsibility as an African-American writer to write this story. He had once said that it was up to him as an African American to put everything he could into his book.[11] Haley told one audience he was obsessed with the writing of a book that would tell everyone in the world that, "Black is beautiful."[12]

To Haley this book was more than a private endeavor. It was a gift to his people—a way he, Alex Haley, could help his race. It would be the kind of accomplishment Simon Haley had hoped his children would someday attain.

Having rejected suicide, Haley returned to his cabin that night and sobbed. Afterward his cloud of despair lifted, and writing poured forth.

As Haley wrote about Africa he felt a closeness developing between Kinte and himself. There were even times when he felt he was the African. He became so involved with his character, that when it came time for Kinte to be captured, Haley couldn't write about it. Instead he wrote on, letting Kinte remain free and adding more and more unplanned pages to his book.

Finally Haley knew he could not put it off any longer—Kinte had to be kidnapped. Writing about

Kinte's enslavement made Haley realize that if he were ever to finish his book, he would have to pull back from his characters and become less attached to them.

The African section of Haley's book was completed at sea. But he was still only one-fourth of the way finished. Doubleday editors were more anxious than ever to get Haley's manuscript. By now they had received many letters from eager readers wondering when Haley's book would be published.

His friend Murray Fisher was the only person who knew how much more work he still had to complete. Fisher later reported, "[Haley] wasn't sure if he'd ever finish, and neither was I."[13]

Haley's editor Lisa Drew seemed to have more faith. According to Haley, Drew "stayed on my case about [the manuscript] and was certainly one of the major factors that helped me get it done."[14]

In 1973 Haley moved to a remote cottage in Jamaica to finish his book. Doubleday had given him what the company called his last advance, and Haley promised to deliver his manuscript in six months. He knew it would take longer.

A few days before the deadline, Haley typed out the first twenty pages of the next section of the book and the book's final pages. Between the beginning and the end, Haley placed more than seven hundred pages of numbered and typewritten research notes. He would take this to Drew, hoping she wouldn't discover he really hadn't written most of the book. This, thought Haley, would give him time to write more.

When Haley handed his manuscript to Drew, he told her that parts of his book still needed a little revising. She read the first few pages, read the final page, then flipped through the pages in between. When she looked up, Haley knew she was satisfied. Quickly he asked Drew for one more advance—which she gave him, along with the promise that it would be the "last penny" Haley received until the book was in final form.[15]

It would be almost two more years before Haley actually finished the book, stalling Doubleday one way or another during that time.

During this time Murray Fisher was a frequent guest of Haley's, and he assisted Haley with his writing. Sometimes Fisher helped Haley plan a scene, sometimes he advised Haley on how to improve a section, and sometimes Fisher actually rewrote Haley's work.[16]

A portion of the book was printed in *Reader's Digest* in 1974. By now Haley had decided on a title. To signify the beginnings of a family tree, Haley would call his book *Roots: The Saga of an American Family.*

In 1976, twelve years from its inception, Haley's book was ready for publication. Because it was the year of America's bicentennial, Haley dedicated it "as a birthday offering to my country."

Doubleday, like Haley, thought this was going to be an important book. In anticipation of big sales, the company printed 200,000 hardback editions. No first edition printing of any book in the United States had been this large. Soon Doubleday would know whether or not this had been wise.

Compliments
and Controversy

Roots: The Saga of an American Family, by Alex Haley, hit the bookstores in October 1976. By January 1977 it was the best-selling nonfiction book in America. Nearly one-half million copies had already been sold.

Haley, who had moved to Los Angeles when he finished the manuscript, spent much of his time traveling around the country promoting *Roots.* Wherever he went crowds greeted him.

The book moved many people. In Los Angeles, where over three thousand people lined up for Haley's autograph, an African-American woman told him, "This is not a book, this is my history."[1]

And a white Californian wrote to Haley, "You have given me a new awareness of your heritage. The people of Africa came alive and with them their beauty, pride, tradition, and strength. Kunta Kinte is now part of me. I will carry him, his family, and his country with me and, hopefully, this new awareness will make me a better human being."[2]

Many book reviewers liked *Roots* too. In *Newsweek* magazine, Paul D. Zimmerman said that Haley had written a book that was "bold in concept" and would "reach millions of people and alter the way we see ourselves."[3]

In the *New York Times Book Review*, Jason Berry wrote, "No other novelist or historian has provided such a shattering, human view of slavery."[4]

But *Roots* drew criticism too. In the *New York Book Review*, Willie Lee Rose wrote that Haley had trouble developing realistic personalities for each of his many characters. The task, she wrote, "challenges Haley the artist, and taxes Haley the historian."[5]

L.L. King wrote in the *Saturday Review*, "*Roots*, unhappily, is not the masterwork one had hoped for."[6]

But in spite of the literary criticism, a new *Roots* project was ready for the public. With Haley's help, prize-winning movie producer David Wolper had made an eight-part miniseries of *Roots* for television.

Like the book, the *Roots* miniseries showed African American history from a black perspective. And, unlike most popular television shows at the time, the movie treated the characters with dignity and intelligence.

The ABC network had originally planned to show

This is the set built to depict Juffure for the television production of *Roots*.

the miniseries over a period of several weeks. But at the last minute, network executives changed their minds. They suddenly feared no one would watch the series. Hoping to command a larger audience, they decided to air the miniseries quickly rather than extend it over many weeks. On eight consecutive nights in January 1977, the miniseries was aired. The executives needn't have worried.

Roots was an unprecedented success! It was estimated that 130 million people watched it—the largest audience any television program had ever had! Many viewers tuned in to all eight episodes, and the miniseries became a social happening. People planned their evenings around *Roots*, restaurants sat empty during the program, and the previous night's episode was discussed all over America by day.

White viewers proclaimed the shows changed the way they thought about black Americans. The response of one nine-year-old girl seemed to echo what many adults were feeling. "I used to not like blacks. Now I feel sorry for them because they were treated like that."[7] *Time* magazine reported that many people felt the miniseries gave them "a more sympathetic view of blacks by giving them a greater appreciation of black history."[8] Some African-American leaders even saw *Roots* as an important civil rights event.

Haley saw the miniseries' success in another way. "The public has a subconscious hunger for something with weight, depth and social value—and they found it on television in *Roots*."[9]

Through *Roots*, the book, Haley had achieved modest fame. But because of the massive television audience that watched the miniseries, Haley shot to stardom. The morning after the first episode, Haley missed a flight when he was mobbed at Kennedy airport by people who wanted his autograph. Scenes such as this were frequently repeated in the months that followed.

The number of fans Haley attracted made it clear that the public loved *Roots*. So did many critics, and the miniseries went on to win six Emmy Awards.

Since September, Haley's book had been winning awards too. One was the prestigious Spingarn Medal from the NAACP, an annual medal given in recognition of an outstanding achievement by an African American. Jackie Robinson, Martin Luther King, Jr., and Langston Hughes were all African Americans who had received the medal in the past. Now Haley was being honored. In addition *Roots* received a tribute from the United States Senate on March 14, 1977.

Then on April 18, 1977, came the news that *Roots* had won a special Pulitzer Prize, one of the most important awards an American author can receive. The award committee felt that the book was an important contribution to the literature of slavery.

Not everyone, though, thought that *Roots* deserved

such praise. Some critics found several aspects of *Roots* historically inaccurate.

First, Haley's portrayal of Juffure as a farming village was incorrect. In the eighteenth century Juffure was a busy trading center, possibly having a population as large as 3,000 people.[10]

Furthermore, because of treaties between African rulers and European slave traders, some historians did not believe any African from Juffure could have been captured and enslaved in 1767.[11]

Writer Willie Lee Rose pointed to other inaccuracies in Haley's text. Among many, she cited how the slaves picked cotton where cotton was never grown and how wire fencing appeared almost one hundred years before its actual use.[12]

In another part of *Roots*, Kinte's foot is cut off as punishment. He survives, living to an old age. But black historian Eric Perkins exerted, "It is well known that slaves did not live after their limbs were severed."[13]

Perkins also argued that Haley's ancestral slaves were house servants, a minority who led privileged lives compared to field hands. Therefore, he said, if Haley wanted to tell the story of the masses, he had chosen the wrong story.[14]

Many people felt that these were trivial concerns in light of what *Roots* had done for race relations in America. But other people believed that Haley, just as

Nineteen-year-old LeVar Burton played the role of the enslaved Kunta Kinte in the television miniseries *Roots*.

anyone who wrote nonfiction, must be held accountable for presenting the truth.

Rose argued that the errors in details made her wonder of the truth "of central matters in which it is important to have full faith."[15]

Haley later acknowledged that there were dozens of errors in *Roots*. Because of the time pressures he was under, he said that *Roots* was not his best writing. The rush to finish the book led to many inaccuracies.[16]

Then came something even more troubling. Margaret Alexander Walker, the director of black studies at Jackson State College in Mississippi, charged that parts of *Roots* had been copied from a book she wrote called *Jubilee*. Walker filed a lawsuit against Haley, but failing to prove her claims, she lost the case.

Then another expert of black culture, Harold Courlander, charged Haley with copying parts of his 1967 novel *The African*. In court Haley said he had never read *The African*. At the end of the trial, however, he admitted that "various materials from *The African* by Harold Courlander had found their way into his book *Roots*."[17]

Haley maintained that using Courlander's work had been accidental. He said that during the long years he had spent researching and writing *Roots*, people sometimes gave him notes that they thought might help him. "I would stick them in my pocket," Haley said, "and when I [got] home, I would dump them all in a box; that's my only explanation of what happened."[18] Haley settled this case out of court for over $500,000.[19]

Haley was dealt another blow when British journalist Mark Ottaway challenged the accuracy of his genealogical work. Ottaway understood that much of the action and dialogue in *Roots* was invented according to what seemed plausible historically. Haley had always referred to this aspect of the book as "faction," a mix of fact and fiction.

What Ottaway questioned was Haley's claim that he had found his African ancestor. Ottaway discovered that Kebba Fofana was not a griot at all. He was, rather, the son of a Muslim priest. As such he was to take over his father's duties upon the elder's death. But the people of Juffure rejected Fofana as their priest. They felt he did not know enough Muslim theology, and he did not conduct himself in a moral manner.[20]

Haley admitted learning in 1973 that Fofana was an unreliable source of information. A letter from a Gambian archivist had informed him that Fofana was not a griot or any kind of oral historian.[21]

When Ottaway asked Haley about these problems, Haley said "he found the African end of his inquiries so confusing, so obscured by contradictory statements from different sources, that he very nearly decided to make the African section, if not the entire book a mere historical novel."[22] He went on to concede that his reliance on

Fofana was perhaps an error and that he may have been misled.

Later, journalist Phillip Nobile charged that Gambian leaders had told Fofana what to say to Haley prior to his visit to Juffure. According to Nobile, Haley knew the Gambian leaders had done this, and he knew what Fofana was going to tell him.[23]

Genealogist Elizabeth Shown Mills and Professor Gary B. Mills wondered how Haley's American lineage held up. Haley had claimed that all of the major incidents, names, and dates he used in his book were true. But to the Mills' dismay, they found that the documents Haley used as evidence of his ancestry did not support the family ties as described in *Roots*.

There were numerous pieces of evidence, in fact, that contradicted Haley's claims. For example, Haley felt sure that the slave named Toby whom he found mentioned in a 1768 document was Kunta Kinte who had arrived on America's shores in 1767. Yet the Mills found this same Toby mentioned in six separate documents over a period of four years preceding 1767. Toby, they concluded, was not Kunta Kinte.

The Mills believed that Haley chose to ignore various written documentation that contradicted the stories he had heard as a child. This, they said, was an error common to amateur genealogists who do not understand how easily family stories become "blurred by time [and] colored by emotion and imagination."[24]

Haley offered no refutations to the Mills' conclusions. To all of the criticisms, he only contended that he wrote *Roots* as a symbolic history of African Americans. He wanted to give his people an identity, a past, a place where their culture and race had begun. Whites had their Garden of Eden, Haley argued, but blacks' history had been obliterated by slavery. "You must understand," Haley told Ottaway, "this book is also symbolic. I, we, need a place called Eden."[25]

Several years later Haley explained how this idea drove him on in his writing. "I was caught up in the sweep, and the swell of the hugeness of the overall thing. The quest for the symbolic history of a people, just swept me like a twig atop a rushing water."[26]

In 1978 Haley said, "Writing a book is very much like having a baby. Once it's published, it takes off and becomes its own entity."[27] *Roots* certainly seemed to have taken on a life of its own.

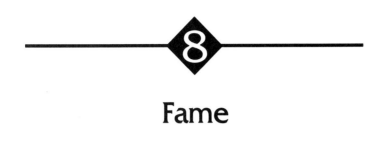

Fame

In spite of challenges regarding *Roots'* authenticity, Haley and his book remained popular. Many people felt that even if Haley had made false claims, his book had done a lot of good. *Roots* had helped white people to better understand African Americans and had made blacks feel better about themselves. Donna Britt, writing in *The Washington Post* summed up these feelings by saying, "Whatever the truth [is], I'm grateful to Haley for having given all African Americans a family tree whose branches stretched clear to Africa."[1]

In addition *Roots* had triggered an appreciation of history and geneaology in all kinds of Americans. Haley had always suspected his book would be popular. "In all of us," he said, "black, brown, white, yellow—there is a desire to make this symbolic journey back to the touchstone of our family."[2]

Still the enormity of the response astounded him. Suddenly he was thrust into the role of contemporary hero. A 1978 poll taken among African-American youths ranked Haley as the third most admired black man in America. Only Muhammad Ali and Stevie Wonder placed ahead of him.

Yet Haley seemed unaffected by the glitter of stardom. Museum director John Rice Irwin tells about the day Haley disappeared while lunching with a group of editors and celebrities. Eventually he was found in the kitchen, signing autographs for the cooks.

But more than making Haley a hero, *Roots* had become a social phenomena. Colleges were teaching classes using the book, newborns were being named Kunta Kinte, and people were pouring into archives around the nation to investigate their own ancestry.

This overwhelming success and popularity, Haley reasoned, must be for a purpose. He told one interviewer, "I never thought of myself as a man with a mission, but if *Roots* has given me one, then I want to make it count."[3]

Haley felt it urgent for African-American children to learn about their ancestry. Knowing about their grandparents' and great-grandparents' fights for freedom and civil rights could instill pride in African-American youth.

As a result of *Roots'* success, Alex Haley became a contemporary hero. Here he is signing autographs after speaking at Hamilton College's 1977 graduation ceremonies.

Unfortunately our society isolates children from the elderly, Haley said, making the passing of family history through storytelling rare. So Haley recommended children ask their grandparents about the family's history and write it down. This written history, plus old photographs and letters, would begin a family archive. A family's past is priceless, Haley said, and without a written history, it could be lost.

In addition to teaching children the family's history, Haley saw grandparents as having another important function. There are "certain things that a grandmammy or a granddaddy can do for a child that no one else can. It's sort of like stardust—the relationship between grandparents and children. The lack of this for many children has to have a negative impact on society. The edges of these children are a little sharper for the lack of it."[4]

Many people seemed to agree with Haley's views, for he was in constant demand on the lecture circuit for the next ten years. His secretary once counted more than eight hundred speaking requests for a single-six month period. One year Haley spent 226 nights in motels!

And these nights were often short ones. Haley's hectic schedule frequently kept him busy from breakfast to midnight, seven days a week. There were interviews, speeches, press conferences, autograph sessions—and the travel to and from. Once Haley was so tired he fell asleep while delivering a speech!

Haley described this new phase of his life as "a whirlpool into which I've fallen."[5] His son William observed that after *Roots* "the world gained a grandfather and I lost a dad."[6]

Haley was besieged by admirers asking him for money, advice, and help with their writing. People followed him home and slipped notes under his door. He was even approached in a restroom one evening by fans requesting his autograph.

Haley still wasn't used to his fame the night six African-American teenagers surrounded him at a convenience store. He wondered what they wanted. Finally the leader stepped forward to ask, "Alex? Could I shake your hand?"[7]

Being a role model to African-American youth was a responsibility Haley took seriously. When one young girl told him, "I'm going to write a bigger book than you," he quickly replied, "Come on, honey, and do it."[8]

It would take quite a book to top *Roots'* success, though. In 1977 *Forbes* magazine estimated that Haley would earn at least five million dollars from the book and miniseries.

But Haley said that the money itself meant little to him. "All I'm concerned with," he said, "is just being comfortable, being able to pay my debts, and having a little margin to buy something or make a gift to somebody."[9] Haley claimed to have no interest in fancy cars or clothes and believed he could again live in his old Greenwich Village apartment if he had to.

In fact there were times when Haley longed for those days—or at least the endless hours he had to write then. Now he rarely wrote, even though he told one interviewer he'd rather be a writer than anything else.

Eventually Haley hoped the *Roots* fervor would die down, and he'd be able to get back to his writing. But the demands on his time never slowed. Finally Haley decided that if he was going to write, he'd have to work where no one could find him.

So he rented a small house in Los Angeles to use as a hideaway. Often he would drive to it from his office, circle the block until no one was around, and then open the garage door electronically. Once inside, he'd quickly close the door and enter the house, where he would write until dawn.

Between 1976 and 1986, Haley published a handful of articles in popular magazines. One was about ex-slave ship captain John Newton. Another was about the people who inhabited a small South Carolina island.

In addition Haley was planning more books. As his next project, he wanted to write a book telling how he had traced his ancestors back to Africa. He would name this book *Search*. In the meantime he produced a two record album that told the story.

Also Haley hoped to complete the manuscript he had set out to write for Doubleday in 1964. Now he was calling it *Home to Henning*. It would tell about life in the small Tennessee town. Haley described this book as stories about "the little people who did whatever they did and died and would never be thought about again if I didn't write about them."[10]

Haley was still active in television too. He wrote a sequel to *Roots* called *Roots: The Next Generation*. The producer of the original *Roots* David Wolper also produced this fourteen-hour miniseries that came to be known as *Roots II*. It was shown in February 1979.

Roots II showed the lives of Haley's ancestors from 1882 through 1967 as they struggled through two world wars, the Great Depression, and racial conflict. The program ended with Haley's life. "Seeing myself on the screen was awesome," he reported. "It wasn't fun watching myself losing my first wife and seeing how I was at fault, but I had to admit that it was true."[11]

After *Roots II* came another program developed by Haley and famous television producer Norman Lear.

Palmerstown, USA was about two friends—one black and one white—growing up in the South in the 1930s. The show revolved around the racial tensions that tested their friendship. The stories for a few of the programs came from Haley's own childhood days in Henning.

Haley never had enough hours to accomplish everything he wanted to do. He rarely had time to visit old friends and missed the leisurely conversations they used to have. He was sure he hurt the feelings of many

Well-known television producer Norman Lear and Haley teamed up to develop a new television show called *Palmerstown, USA.*

when he told them he was too busy to visit. And though he made frequent phone calls to his children, there was never enough time for them either.

Success had benefitted both Haley and America. He would never want to change that. But at times, his loss of privacy frustrated him. Once he remarked, "I hope to God I never have anything like the success of *Roots* happen to me again."[12]

There were, however, a few quirks to success Haley did enjoy. For one, it opened to him a world of fascinating and powerful personalities. To Haley, meeting people such as President Jimmy Carter, Queen Farah of Iran, and Elizabeth Taylor was a "fantasy come true."[13]

Another benefit to success was having the money to pursue the projects in which he was interested. Haley could now reactivate the Kinte Foundation that he had originally begun in 1972 with his brother George.

The Kinte Foundation was to be an archive of genealogical material for African Americans. It would house a variety of records such as church rolls, slave lists, wills, personal letters, and diaries. These documents would be available to anyone wanting to research his or her ancestry.

Wealth also allowed Haley to undertake another dream. In 1983 he bought a farm near Norris, Tennessee. The farmhouse, which sat on 120 acres of land, had originally been built in the 1830s. It had no plumbing or electricity. Haley renovated the house, retaining its old-fashioned charm but adding modern conveniences. He came to refer to it as "Granny's house with a microwave."[14]

The farm was a peaceful place, a restful change from Haley's hectic life. He wished he could spend more time there. And he delighted in sharing it with friends who sometimes stayed for months at a time.

Eventually Haley added three large guest houses to his property and converted an old log barn into a meeting hall. The farm would become a retreat where creative and innovative people of all races and nationalities could relax and exchange ideas.

Some of Haley's famous guests included Oprah Winfrey, Lou Gossett, Jr., Mike Wallace, Brooke Shields, Maya Angelou, and Dr. C. Eric Lincoln.

In 1986 Haley was honored by the State of Tennessee when it bought Will and Cynthia Palmer's house in Henning from the Haley brothers. This was the house Alex Haley called home; the house where he had spent Sunday afternoons listening to his mother play the piano and summer evenings hearing family stories.

The state painstakingly restored the Palmer home to its original condition. On November 20, 1986, it was officially opened as The Alex Haley State Historical Site and Museum. The museum is the only state-owned historic site in Tennessee devoted to African-American history. Alex, George, and Julius Haley all attended the opening ceremony. Tennessee Governor Lamar Alexander was there too.

The Haley House Museum looks much the same now as it did when Haley lived there. In the kitchen is an old-fashioned cookstove, and the Palmer family's royal blue china. Bertha's piano still stands in the parlor, holding the music she played sixty years ago. Looking carefully, one can see Bertha's signature atop the sheets of music.

Displayed throughout the house are photographs, artifacts, and memorabilia from Haley's family. Museum interpreters tell about Haley's ancestors and his struggle as an author. Fred Montgomery, a frequent museum interpreter, reminisces about his boyhood days in the Palmer home.

Other interpreters tell what life was like in the rural south in the early 1900s. They explain lye soap-making, sausage grindings, and "Poor Man's Pudding." During the summer the museum sometimes presents a story hour for children. Then the interpreters dress in clothes from the era to tell youngsters a tale.

Attending the opening of his old home was an event Haley would not have missed. But Haley's nonstop schedule of speaking engagements, television projects, and writing was exacting a toll on his health. In 1987 his hectic schedule put him in the hospital.

A Turtle Atop a Fencepost

The doctor's diagnosis was exhaustion, and Haley knew that if he were to stay healthy, his lifestyle would have to change. He decided to quit lecturing. "You make a lot of money, but it doesn't mean anything when you're never still long enough to enjoy it or to work creatively."[1]

He moved from Los Angeles to Knoxville, Tennessee, to live with his old friend, George Sims.

At the time he was married to Myran Lewis whom he had met while working on the *Roots* movie. His wife stayed in Los Angeles where she worked as a television writer. Though she and Haley were on friendly terms, they preferred to live separately, each free to pursue his or her own career.

Another Wolper/Haley television project aired in

December 1988. The program was called *The Gift* and featured characters from the original *Roots* miniseries.

But writing was what Haley wanted to do, and he had not published a book for eleven years. Referring to writing, he had once said,

> There's nothing I'd rather do, except perhaps be a surgeon. In many ways it's similar delicate, careful work, and I act like a surgeon. When I'm writing I take six showers a day, and wash my hands maybe twenty times. And it's a physical thing with me. When it's going well, I find myself tapping my foot in rhythm with the keys, as if there's a cadence going. I like to do first drafts at night, when I'm tired, and then do the surgical work in the morning when I'm sharp—and I love writing on a ship at sea. In fact, if I had my druthers, I'd spend half the year at sea.[2]

When an editor at Doubleday challenged Haley to write a short novel in thirty days, Haley took up the gauntlet. He booked passage on a freighter going to Australia, and aboard ship he wrote twelve hours a day. He finished a novel before the end of his trip, winning the bet. *A Different Kind of Christmas* was published in 1988.

In *A Different Kind of Christmas*, Haley wove a fictional tale around historical fact. The main character Fletcher Randall is the son of a southern plantation owner. When Randall goes north to college, he befriends three Quakers who show him something he's never thought about before—the inhumanity of slavery. In time Randall becomes an agent of the Underground Railroad and is asked to betray his own parents and their way of life.

Armed with research notes and half-written manuscripts, Haley now boarded freighters as often as possible to write. At sea he wrote from dusk until daybreak, feeling that, "The quiet allows you to get to be one with whatever you're working on."[3]

Wealth gave Haley the freedom to write about things that excited him. One of his favorite projects was *Home to Henning*. George Sims, who had lived in the Tennessee town longer than Haley, came up with some of the story ideas Haley wrote.[4]

Haley also planned a book about Madam C. J. Walker, the daughter of black sharecroppers. Madam Walker became a millionaire by producing and marketing hair care products for African Americans. She donated much of her money to various African-American causes. Haley believed, "Madam played an amazing role in the advancement of blacks, much more than is commonly recognized."[5]

Haley and the African-American musician and composer, Quincy Jones, discussed writing Madam Walker's story into a musical play for Broadway.

Another book idea developed because Haley's father "always wanted to know why I didn't write about his side of the family."[6] Many years earlier Haley had learned that his paternal great-grandfather was a white southerner named James Jackson, Jr.

Jackson raped one of his slaves, a woman named Easter. Haley knew that as horrible as it was, rape by white masters happened to slaves every day. Easter bore a child and named her Queen.

Queen grew up a slave and at the end of the Civil War set out on her own. After several years of poverty and strife, she married sharecropper Alec Haley. Alec and Queen had children, one being a boy named Simon who loved to learn. When Simon grew up, he had sons of his own, and he named one Alex Haley.

Haley had always wanted to pay tribute to his grandmother Queen. Because of her, his father had been allowed to go to school instead of staying home to work on the farm. In those days a son who did not help work on the farm was considered "wasted."

While researching this book Haley visited the Alabama plantation where Queen Jackson had lived. As he walked around the Jackson family cemetery, a white family stopped to look at their ancestors' graves. Trying to be helpful, one of the group pointed and told Haley, "The slave graveyard is over there."[7]

They were astonished when Haley replied, "No, I think my relative is James Jackson, Jr."[8] Then Haley explained why he was there.

One of Haley's objectives in writing about Queen was to show how African Americans and white

Near the end of his life, Haley began research for a book that would tell the story of this woman, Queen Haley.

Americans have closer bloodlines than what is commonly thought. In spite of varied skin colors, many are related. In Haley's words: "Can you imagine what the understanding of that can do to help knit our society together. What brings people closer together than family?"[9]

During this time Haley still published occasional articles in national magazines. One was about his struggle to become an author. Another was about the man who donated money to help his father finish college.

Haley also wrote political and social commentaries regarding racism. Though discrimination was illegal, Haley knew racism survived. Reports such as the one in a national news magazine that told of an epidemic of ethnic hatred sweeping the world deeply disturbed Haley.

Especially disconcerting, Haley thought, were the accounts of racism on America's college campuses—the place where the nation's greatest minds were supposed to be developing.

Haley was also upset by subtle racism: racism that was hard to see. He believed that subtle racism was even more dangerous than overt racism because not everyone recognized it. But several facts convinced Haley it existed. For instance Haley cited a statistic that reported more African-American men of college age in prison

After a life of considerable hardship, Queen married Alec Haley, a Tennessee farmer.

than in college. It depressed Haley that so many bright minority men were behind bars.

Haley believed that crime by youth was caused by the lack of educational skills such as reading and writing. With no education black youth have little chance for success Haley argued, so they turn to crime. Said Haley,

> One of the legacies of slavery, followed by legal discrimination and separation of races, is a people mostly educationally impaired. America desperately needs a better educated workforce. To help develop the huge positive potential of blacks to improve this work force, we need affirmative-action scholarships. And until there is an equitably and competitively educated work force, we need affirmative-action jobs.[10]

Three decades earlier, Malcolm X had told Haley he resented the way white America wasted the talents of blacks. This same thing concerned Haley now, and he was determined to bring about whatever changes he could.

So Haley donated money and time to projects that promoted education, most notably adult literacy programs and programs that encouraged youth to remain in school. In addition, each year Haley gave two top high school students from Henning full scholarships to a Tennessee college. One scholarship went to a white student and the other to a black. "I do it for both black and white because my father was helped by a white benefactor and so it would seem only correct that at some point some of us would be able to return the favor."[11]

Haley gave to other kinds of charities as well. Among them were the National Alliance for Mental Health and the Memphis St. Jude Children's Research Hospital. "There is a saying about people who have achieved a position," Haley said. "Anytime you see a turtle atop a fence post, you know it had some help."[12]

Haley likened himself to that turtle. Had it not been for the man who paid for his father's last year of college, Haley may have been a sharecropper's son destined to a life of hard work and poverty. Instead he had grown up a professor's son surrounded by books and opportunities to better himself in a chosen field. Now Haley felt it was his turn to give to others.

Unfortunately Haley's generosity drained his income. "He never had it in him to say no," his brother George said.[13] To keep up with his charitable donations, Haley returned to public speaking. Though he never resumed the hectic schedule of his post-*Roots* days, he did give about fifty lectures a year.

Occasionally he talked at prisons or schools. One of Haley's favorite topics was education. He felt it was wrong for high schools to graduate students who could not read or write. He also addressed the importance of multicultural education. Haley hoped that when teachers taught American history, they discussed the diverse cultures that contributed to making America.

"The truth is," Haley said, "you can't know American history if you do not know the role played by Black people, by Native Americans, or by Orientals. The history of America is mixed history. We desperately need to have a better awareness, knowledge of, and respect for each other's contributions."[14]

At his lectures people sometimes asked how to become writers. He would say that first and foremost, writers must have self-discipline. For instance Haley couldn't wait until he was inspired to write. Because of his busy schedule, he had to write whenever time allowed. But more than this, writers need the discipline to push themselves to excellence, even when others did not push them.

Haley usually rewrote his own work several times before he was satisfied with it. First he typed his story in rough form, just getting his idea down. At this point, he said it was usually so bad he wouldn't show it to anyone. The important thing was getting it down on paper.

Next Haley revised his work slowly and carefully, using a green ink pen. After retyping it, he revised it again, and frequently repeated this process two more times before a piece was ready to go to a publisher.

Through this revision process, Haley allowed his own voice to come through. He advised people to develop their own styles instead of trying to imitate another writer. "As long as you're trying to be like someone else, you're not being yourself, and hence, whatever your style is, it's not natural. Your style is that which is natural to you."[15]

Haley encouraged young people who wanted to write, but he cautioned them that there was a big difference between wanting to be a writer and writing. "You've got to want to write, not want to be a writer," he said.[16]

Finally Haley said, a writer must be determined. "I have a favorite made-up statistic that of every thousand people who set out to write, only one will become a professional writer. The others will fall out along the way in the face of constant rejection. To make it as a writer, you have to have the same kind of quality that lets water roll off a duck's back. If you quit, you may as well have never begun."[17]

Haley had never quit and had a wealth of research material, letters, rough drafts, and completed manuscripts to prove it. He had once described himself as a pack rat, but now he gave up much of what he had saved over the years.

In 1991 Haley announced he was donating his papers to the University of Tennessee on the condition that nothing be opened to the public until after his death. His working material was boxed and sent to the University. Haley had planned to help the archivists at the university organize his material. But he never had the chance.

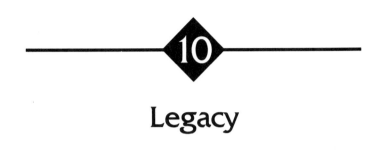

Legacy

In February 1992 Haley traveled to Washington to speak at a United States Naval base near Seattle. He was to lecture employees at the base and address students at a local high school. Both speeches were to focus on interracial harmony.

But before his appearances, Haley fell ill and was taken to a hospital in Seattle. There, just after midnight on February 10, he died of cardiac arrest.

Haley left behind friends of all colors from everywhere in the world. Several of them gathered in Memphis, Tennessee, on February 15 to say their good-byes. Attallah Shabazz (Malcolm X's daughter), Maya Angelou, and Gambian Ambassador Ousman A. Sallah were among the many who eulogized Haley there.

The service ended with an African chant that Quincy Jones had adapted into song.

A cold wind blew through Henning the day Alex Haley came home for the last time. A funeral was held in the Christian Methodist Episcopal Church. To honor his old friend, Fred Montgomery sang a spiritual. And African-American civil rights leader Jesse Jackson spoke, saying Haley "lit up the long night of slavery. He gave our grandparents personhood. He gave *Roots* to the rootless."[1]

After the funeral, people crowded into the streets to follow the hearse to the Haley House Museum, where a musician dressed in African clothes drummed. Then Coast Guard pall bearers carried Haley's casket to the burial site on the lawn. As mourners sang "Amazing Grace," the casket was lowered into the ground. Then Gambian soil mixed with the soil of Tennessee was thrown onto it.

For several days people poured into Henning to visit Haley's grave. Most had never met him, but felt as if they knew him from his work that had deeply touched their lives.

Haley's books, which represented and outlived the turbulent times from which they grew, were still meaningful to people. *The Autobiography of Malcolm X* had become a contemporary classic with its unique perspective on poverty in America, the 1960s, and

African-American history. And *Roots* still inspired people of all backgrounds to feel proud of their own heritage.

As one who had risen to fame and fortune from humble beginnings, Haley had been an important role model to many African Americans. He had won the prestigious Pulitzer Prize and the NAACP's Spingarn Award. In addition Haley had received thirty-seven honorary doctorates, including one from Elizabeth City Teacher's College and another from the United States Coast Guard Academy.

But besides these academic honors, Haley had achieved material success. More that six million copies of both *The Autobiography of Malcolm X* and *Roots* were sold. Haley had also made money from his television endeavors.

Therefore it was surprising news when Haley's brother George revealed his estate to be one and one-half million dollars in debt. Much of this was money Haley owed on his farm.

George wanted to pay his brother's debts and clear the estate. So he decided to sell the farm and all of Haley's possessions, then use the cash from the sales to pay back what was owed.

Researchers set about assembling and organizing Haley's belongings. Among his papers they found various notes, letters, and manuscripts that he had not donated to the University of Tennessee. One manuscript, an unpublished musical called *The Way*, focused on the senselessness of interracial struggle. A working manuscript for *Roots* was also found.

Another manuscript researchers came across was a version of *The Autobiography of Malcolm X* that contained the four unpublished and previously unknown sections of the book. Finally there were the two novels Haley had been working on at the time of his death: *Home to Henning* and *Queen.*

Selling any of Haley's possessions seemed wrong to some people. Haley's friend Quincy Jones said, "It kills me that [Haley who was] so wrapped in history is in jeopardy of having his life scattered all over."[2] Henry Louis Gates, Jr., of Harvard noted that "The black literary legacy is already so fragmented that willful fragmentation is incredibly disturbing."[3]

But George Haley didn't agree. "My brother's legacy cannot be lost," he said. "It's forever available to anyone who can walk into a library."[4]

Practicality drove George, and he wanted to pay the debts as soon as possible. So in October 1992 he held an auction to sell what he could of his brother's belongings. Though the farm was not sold until nearly a year later, the auction did sell many Haley items.

George Jewett, a friend of Haley's from San Francisco, bought his Pulitzer Prize for $50,000. He then donated it to the Haley House Museum.

A collector of African-American books named Bill Shaw bought the working draft of *Roots* for $75,000.

The manuscript of *The Autobiography of Malcolm X* was purchased by Gregory J. Reed, an attorney from Detroit. Reed paid $110,000 for the manuscript that contained handwritten comments by both Malcolm X and Haley. "One of my missions," Reed later said, "was to preserve Malcolm's work."[5] He hoped to loan the complete manuscript to interested institutions.

Possibly the most sentimental item for sale was Haley's sardine and coin plaque. Jewett purchased it for $10,000 and donated it to the State Museum of Tennessee with the stipulation that it be displayed at the Haley House Museum.

Another buyer at the auction was the University of Tennessee. A university representative purchased materials to add to Knoxville's Haley collection. One item he bought was Haley's diary from 1961 and 1962.[6] Added to the work Haley had already donated, the University of Tennessee's collection became the largest repository of Haley material.

On February 23, 1993, a ceremony was held to officially open this collection. George Haley was present to express his satisfaction that much of his brother's materials were collected in a Tennessee library.

In addition to the opening of the Haley collection, another event relevant to Alex Haley occurred in February. This was the airing of *Queen*, the third miniseries based on the lives of Haley's ancestors. A writer named David Stevens had written the movie scripts and Haley had read and approved them.

The three-part movie was introduced with the following words: "Here is [Queen's] story as Haley would have wanted it told. And it is to his memory that this miniseries is dedicated."

Queen told the story of Queen Jackson Haley, Haley's paternal grandmother whose mother was a black slave and father was a white plantation owner. As she grew, Queen became a house servant who played a major role in keeping the plantation running during and immediately after the Civil War.

The movie told the same story as the book *Queen*, which was now published. David Stevens had written it too, using Haley's research notes and outline. Unlike *Roots*, *Queen* was labeled fiction because the family stories from which the book was developed could not be verified.[7]

Researchers soon discovered one major difference between reality and the book—Queen's age. Though the Queen in the book was a young woman at the start of the Civil War, the real Queen was born just three years before it began.[8]

The year 1993 had begun as a momentous one to the memory of Alex Haley. The opening of the Haley collection at the University of Tennessee, the broadcast of *Queen*, and the publication of the book were all events of great importance. But amid these came a startling article written in the *Village Voice* magazine.

In it, writer Phillip Nobile charged that Haley had used trickery and deceit to make it look as if he had found his African ancestors. Nobile believed *Roots* had been built on a foundation of lies. Though Haley's family and friends strongly denied the charges, Nobile's article raised enough disturbing questions to send shock waves through the academic world.

The American Society of Journalists and Authors who had just decided to call some of its awards the Alex Haley Awards, changed its mind. The organization would now name them something else.[9] There was even talk of rescinding Haley's Pulitzer Prize.[10]

Genealogist Elizabeth Shown Mills worried that until the general public understood that *Roots* was largely fiction, the integrity of genealogy would be compromised. In her words, " . . . myth is myth, fiction is fiction." Furthermore, " . . . plagiarism and the falsification of research results are just as reprehensible in [genealogy] as they are in every other field of scholarly inquiry."[11]

Mills had another concern. Haley's claims to have found his African ancestors aroused false hopes in others wishing to do the same. Eager to learn their lineage, these people became targets for swindlers ready to present them with useless or inaccurate information—for a fee.

According to Mills, the ancestry of African Americans could be researched through written records rather than less reliable oral accounts. As evidence of such, she cited one study by Johni Cerny that traced comedian Bill Cosby's paternal line to Maria Cosby, a slave born in about 1797, and another by C. Bernard Ruffin III who traced his family roots through slavery to the 1760s.[12]

Still Haley supporters steadfastly believed he was an honorable man who had painstakingly reasearched, verified, and reported the family stories he had heard at his grandmother's knee.

A third group believed that Haley had accurately documented some of his story, but knowingly filled in missing pieces with fiction.

Curtis Lyons, former curator of the University of Tennessee Haley collection, wasn't sure there would ever be definitive answers regarding Haley's methods and motives in writing *Roots*. He stated, "I honestly don't believe that we will ever really know the answers to a lot of the questions about *Roots* and Haley."[13]

But time may yield new information. Until then, Alex Haley's final place in American history and literature has yet to be decided. But one thing is certain—his two most celebrated works, *The Autobiography of Malcolm X* and *Roots,* ushered in a new consciousness in America.

The Autobiography of Malcolm X gave validity to the

In 1989 Haley posed on the porch of his Tennessee farmhouse.

anger felt by millions of mistreated Americans. Contemporary filmmaker Spike Lee called the work, "The most important book I'll ever read. It changed the way I thought; it changed the way I acted. It has given me courage that I didn't know I had inside me. I'm one of hundreds of thousands whose life changed for the better."[14]

Roots introduced America to a new perspective about its own history. As Donna Britt, writing in *The Washington Post* pointed out: "In the land of the free, at least forty million men, women and children, like those that Alex Haley may have fictionalized, lived and died without ever belonging to themselves. All of America needed to know them. More than anyone, Alex Haley made the introduction."[15]

It was Alex Haley's hope that his writing would bring people closer together and make a difference in the world. Perhaps his greatest wish was for the message of his books to endure.

"The question is," he had once remarked, "what did we leave behind? I feel great knowing I will have left my books."[16]

Chronology

1921—Alex Haley is born in Ithaca, New York

1925—Begins school in Henning, Tennessee

1931—Moves to Normal, Alabama

1932—Mother Bertha dies

1936—Graduates from high school in Normal, Alabama

1937—Enters Alcorn A. & M. College, in Lorman, Mississippi

1938—Enters Elizabeth City Teacher's College, North Carolina

1939—Enlists in United States Coast Guard

1943 Is assigned to the U.S.S. *Murzim*; writes letters
-1944—for shipmates

1949—Is promoted to Chief Journalist

1950—First article is published in *This Week* magazine

1959—Retires from Coast Guard; moves to Greenwich Village

1965—*The Autobiography of Malcolm X* is published

1967—Takes first trip to Africa

1973—Moves to Jamaica to finish *Roots*

1976—*Roots* is published; moves to Los Angeles

1988—*A Different Kind of Christmas* is published; moves to Tennessee

1992—Alex Haley dies in Seattle, Washington

1993—*Queen* is published

Chapter Notes

Chapter 1

1. Alex Haley, "The Shadowland of Dreams," *Reader's Digest*, August 1991, pp. 83-85.

2. Ibid.

3. Alex Haley, "In Search of 'The African'," *American History Illustrated*, February 1974, pp. 21-32.

4. Ibid.

5. Alex Haley, "We Must Honor Our Ancestors," *Ebony*, November 1990, pp. 152-156.

6. Haley, "In Search of 'The African'," pp. 21-32.

7. *Current Biography* (New York: H.W. Wilson, 1977), p. 186.

8. Marilyn Kern-Foxworth, *Dictionary of Literary Biography*, Volume 38 (Detroit: Gale Research Company, 1985), p. 116.

9. *Current Biography*, p. 186.

10. Nada Beth Glick and Filomena Simora, eds., *Bowker Annual of Library and Book Trade Information Twenty-third Edition*, (New York: R.R. Bowker, 1978), p. 434.

11. "Why *Roots* Hit Home," *Time*, February 14, 1977, pp. 69-75.

12. Deirdre Carmody, "Haley Gets Special Pulitzer Prize; Lufkin, Tex., News Takes a Medal," *New York Times*, April 19, 1977, p. 44:1.

13. Haley, "The Shadowland of Dreams," pp. 83-85.

14. Ibid.

15. Haley, "In Search of 'The African'," pp. 21-32.

Chapter 2

1. Alex Haley, "The Man on the Train," *Reader's Digest*, February 1991, pp. 55-58.

2. Alex Haley, "The Christmas That Gave Me *Roots*," *McCall's*, December 1983, pp. 117, 151-152.

3. "Haley Says Family Gift Inspired Him to Be Writer," *Jet*, October 22, 1990, p. 20.

4. Deposition in The United States District Court for the Northern District of Alabama Southern Division, September 19, 1990.

5. Alex Haley, Introduction to "I Have A Dream" Collection of United States Postage Stamps 1992.

6. Telephone interview.

7. W. McGuire and M. S. Clayton, eds., "An Interview with Alex Haley," *Today's Education*, September 1977, pp. 46-47.

8. Ibid.

9. Ibid.

Chapter 3

1. Public Information Article, Fifth Coast Guard District Office, "Alex Haley . . . Most Unforgettable Character," undated.

2. Alex Haley, "The Most Unforgettable Character I've Met," *Reader's Digest*, March 1961, pp. 73-77.

3. "Why *Roots* Hit Home," pp. 69-75.

4. *Current Biography*, p. 185.

5. "New York Newsmen Pay Glowing Tribute to Coast Guard's Only Chief Journalist," *Coast Guard Magazine*, March 1950, p. 34.

6. Jeffrey Elliot, "The Roots of Alex Haley's Writing Career," *Writer's Digest*, August 1980, pp. 20-27, 47, 53.

7. Ibid.

8. Ibid.

9. Haskel Frankel, "Interviewing the Interviewer," *Saturday Review*, February 5, 1966, pp. 37-38.

Chapter 4

1. Elliot, "The Roots of Alex Haley's Writing Career," pp. 20-27, 47, 53.

2. Alex Haley, "Mr. Muhammad Speaks," *Reader's Digest*, March 1960, pp. 100-104.

3. Ibid.

4. Playboy Editors, *Playboy Interviews* (Chicago, Ill.: HMH Publishing, 1967), p. 37.

5. Ibid., p. 50.

6. Alex Haley, "In 'Uncle Tom' Are Our Guilt and Hope," *New York Times Magazine*, March 1, 1964, pp. 27, 90.

7. Address by Alex Haley to the National Education Association in Philadelphia, Penn., 1972.

8. Alex Haley, "Alex Haley Remembers," *Essence*, November 1983, pp. 52-54, 118, 122.

9. Alex Haley, *The Autobiography of Malcolm X* (New York: Ballantine Books, 1965), p. 387.

10. Michael Silence, "The Haley Papers," *Knoxville News Sentinel*, September 10, 1992, p. A1, A5.

11. Haley, "Alex Haley Remembers," pp. 52-54, 118, 122.

12. Marshall Frady, "The Children of Malcolm," *The New Yorker*, October 12, 1992, pp. 64-81.

13. Haley, *The Autobiography of Malcolm X*, p. 431.

14. Ibid., p. 456.

15. Betty Winston Baye, "Alex Haley's Roots Revisited," *Essence*, February 1992, pp. 88-92.

16. *Current Biography*, p. 185.

17. Ibid.

18. "Text Malcolm X Edited Found in Writer's Estate," *New York Times*, September 11, 1992, p. C:25.

Chapter 5

1. J. D. Podolsky and Civia Tamarkin, "Torn Up by the Roots," *People Weekly*, October 5, 1992, pp. 71-72.

2. McGuire and Clayton, pp. 46-47.

3. Ann Crawford, "A Personal Remembrance of Alex Haley," *Military Living*, March 1992, pp. 3, 6.

4. Haley, *The Autobiography of Malcolm X*, p. 162.

5. "Playboy Interview: Martin Luther King," *Playboy*, January 1965, pp. 347-383.

6. Murray Fisher, "Playboy Interview: Alex Haley," *Playboy*, January 1977, pp. 57-79, 92.

7. Playboy editors, *Playboy Interviews*, p. 31.

8. Frankel, pp. 37-38.

9. Dave Dudajek, "Alex Haley's Local Roots," *Observer Dispatch*, February 11, 1992 p. C:1.

10. Alex Haley, *Roots* (Garden City, N.Y.: Doubleday, 1976), p. 675.

11. Charles L. Todd, "Alex Haley on Campus," *Family Heritage*, October 1978, pp. 131-133.

12. "*Roots* Took Shape at Hamilton, Ex Teacher Haley Tells Grads," *Buffalo Evening News*, June 3, 1977, p. 5.

13. William La Rue, "Alex Haley's Roots Spread from Ithaca throughout CNY," *Syracuse Herald*, February 14, 1993, pp. 3-4.

14. "*Roots* Took Shape at Hamilton, Ex Teacher Haley Tells Grads," p. 5.

15. La Rue, pp. 3-4.

Chapter 6

1. Haley, "In Search of 'The African'," pp. 21-32.

2. Haley, *Roots*, p. 679.

3. Cheryl Forbes, "From These 'Roots'," *Christianity Today*, May 6, 1977, pp. 19-22.

4. Todd, "Alex Haley on Campus," pp. 131-133.

5. Phillip Nobile, "Uncovering *Roots*," *Village Voice*, February 23, 1993, pp. 31-38.

6. Todd, pp. 131-133.

7. Fisher, "Playboy Interview: Alex Haley," pp. 57-79, 92.

8. Hans J. Massaquoi, "Alex Haley: The Man Behind *Roots*," *Ebony*, April 1977, pp. 33-41.

9. Betty Winston Baye, "Alex Haley's Roots Revisited," *Essence*, February 1992, pp. 88-92.

10. Paul D. Zimmerman, "In Search of a Heritage," *Newsweek*, September 27, 1976, pp. 94-96.

11. Haley, "In Search of 'The African'," pp. 21-32.

12. Address by Alex Haley to the National Education Association in Philadelphia, Penn., 1972.

13. Murray Fisher, "In Memoriam: Alex Haley," *Playboy*, July 1992, pp. 161-162.

14. Jane Ammeson, "Rich Heritage Provides Ample Literary Fodder for Alex Haley," *Northwest Compass Readings Magazine*, January 1992, pp. 70-76.

15. Fisher, "*Playboy* Interview: Alex Haley," pp. 57-79, 92.

16. Nobile, "Uncovering *Roots*," pp. 31-38.

Chapter 7

1. Alex Haley, "What *Roots* Means to Me," *Reader's Digest*, May 1977, pp. 73-76.

2. Ibid.

3. Zimmerman, pp. 94-96.

4. *Current Biography*, p. 186.

5. Willie Lee Rose, "An American Family," *New York Review of Books*, November 11, 1976, pp. 3-4, 6.

6. J. Samudio and M.T. Mooney, eds., *Book Review Digest* (New York: H.W. Wilson Company, 1976), p. 489.

7. Harry F. Waters, "After Haley's Comet," *Newsweek*, February 14, 1977, pp. 97-98.

8. "Why *Roots* Hit Home," pp. 69-75.

9. Waters, pp. 97-98.

10. Rose, pp. 3-4, 6.

11. Mark Ottaway, "Tangled Roots," *The Sunday Times*, April 10, 1977, pp. 17, 21.

12. Rose, pp. 3-4, 6.

13. Phillip Nobile, "Haley's *Roots* Is Eroding Under Attacks," *Gadsden Times*, May 16, 1977, p. 4.

14. Ibid.

15. Rose, pp. 3-4, 6.

16. Elliot, "The Roots of Alex Haley's Writing Career," pp. 20-27, 47, 53.

17. "Haley Settles Plagiarism Suit, Concedes Passages," *Publisher's Weekly*, December 25, 1978, p. 22.

18. "*Roots* Was Not All Haley's," *San Francisco Chronicle*, December 15, 1978, pp. 1, 26.

19. Nobile, "Uncovering *Roots*," pp. 31-38.

20. Ottaway, pp. 17, 21.

21. Gerald Fraser, "Haley Is Hoping to Debate Reporter," *New York Times*, April 10, 1977, p. 129.

22. Ottaway, pp. 17, 21.

23. Nobile, "Uncovering *Roots*," pp. 31-38.

24. Gary. B. and Elizabeth Shown Mills, "Roots and the New 'Faction'," *The Virginia Magazine*, January 1981, pp. 3-26.

25. Ottaway, p. 17, 21.

26. Nobile, "Uncovering *Roots*," pp. 31-38.

27. Jeffrey Elliot, "Alex Haley Talks to Jeffrey Elliot," *Negro History Bulletin*, January 1978, pp. 782-789.

Chapter 8

1. Donna Britt, "Rooting Up Haley's Legacy," *The Washington Post*, March 2, 1993, pp. B:1, 4.

2. Haley, "What *Roots* Means to Me," pp. 73-76.

3. Genevieve Millet Landau, "Alex Haley on Kids in Search of Their Roots," *Parents' Magazine*, September 1977, pp. 60-61, 85, 98, 100.

4. "Why *Roots* Hit Home," pp. 69-75.

5. "View from the Whirlpool," *Time*, February 19, 1979, p. 88.

6. LaRue, pp. 3, 4.

7. Elliot, "The Roots of Alex Haley's Writing Career," pp. 20-27, 47, 53.

8. "Why *Roots* Hit Home," pp. 69-75.

9. Massaquoi, pp. 33-41.

10. Patricia Freeman and Jane Sanderson, "Having Left L.A. to Settle in His Native Tennessee, Alex Haley Turns Out His First Book Since *Roots*," *People*, December 12, 1988, pp. 126-128.

11. "View from the Whirlpool," p. 88.

12. Elliot, "The Roots of Alex Haley's Writing Career," pp. 20-27, 47, 53.

13. Alex Haley, "There Are Days When I Wish It Hadn't Happened," *Playboy*, March 1979, pp. 14, 136, 212-216.

14. Freeman and Sanderson, pp. 126-128.

Chapter 9

1. Freeman and Sanderson, pp. 126-128.

2. John F. Baker, "Alex Haley," *Publisher's Weekly*, September 6, 1976, pp. 8, 9, 12.

3. Baye, "Alex Haley's Roots Revisited," pp. 88-92.

4. Nobile, "Uncovering *Roots*," pp. 31-38.

5. Baye, pp. 88-92.

6. Ibid.

7. Rod Dreher, "'Queen' Gambit," *Washington, D.C. Times*, February 14, 1993, p. D:1.

8. Ibid.

9. John Seigenthaler, "Alex Haley's Bramble Amid the Roots," *Tennessean*, February 23, 1992, p. 1D.

10. Alex Haley, "Ideas with a Payoff for Us All," *Time*, July 15, 1991, special advertising section.

11. Ammeson, pp. 70-76.

12. "A Turtle Atop a Fencepost," *U.S. News & World Report*, February 24, 1992, pp. 20-21.

13. Podolsky and Tamarkin, pp. 71-72.

14. "Haley Blasts Debate over Methods of Teaching Black History in U.S. Schools," *Jet*, November 25, 1991, p. 22.

15. Elliot, "The Roots of Alex Haley's Writing Career," pp. 20-27, 47, 53.

16. Haley, "The Shadowland of Dreams," pp. 83-85.

17. Elliot, "The Roots of Alex Haley's Writing Career," pp. 20-27, 47, 53.

Chapter 10

1. Fisher, "In Memoriam: Alex Haley," pp. 161-162.

2. Podolsky and Tamarkin, pp. 71-72.

3. Anders Wenngren, "The Talk of the Town—Family Ties," *The New Yorker*, October 26, 1992, pp. 33-34.

4. Ibid.

5. Telephone interview.

6. Tom Sharp, "Many of Haley's Possessions Will be in Public Domain," Associated Press, October 6, 1992.

7. Esther B. Fein, "Book Notes," *New York Times*, March 3, 1993, p. C:18.

8. 1900 Census of Hardin County, Tennessee, Enumeration District 33, sheet 1. Savannah, hh#3.

9. David R. Zimmerman, "Misplaced Honor," *American Society of Journalists and Authors Newsletter*, May 1993, pp. 11-12.

10. Phillip Nobile, "Uncovering Roots," *Village Voice*, February 23, 1993, pp. 31-88.

11. Telephone conversation on March 7, 1994, with Elizabeth Shown Mills Editor of *National Genealogical Society Quarterly*.

12. Johni Cerny, "From Maria to Bill Cosby: A Case Study in Tracing Black Slave Ancestry," *National Genealogical Society Quarterly*, March 1987, pp. 5-14.

13. Personal correspondence, August 1993.

14. Haley, *The Autobiography of Malcolm X*, book cover.

15. Britt, pp. B:1,4.

16. Alan Carter, "The Roots of His Success," *New York Daily News*, December 7, 1988, pp. 37,40.

Further Reading

If you would like to read Alex Haley's books or learn more about African-American history, here are some books you might find in your local library:

Alvarez, Joseph A. *From Reconstruction to Revolution: The Blacks Struggle for Equality.* New York: Atheneum, 1971.

Durham, Michael S. *Powerful Days: The Civil Rights Photography of Charles Moore.* New York: Stewart, Tabori and Chang, 1991.

Haley, Alex. *The Autobiography of Malcolm X.* New York: Ballantine Books, 1992.

Haley, Alex. *A Different Kind of Christmas.* New York: Doubleday, 1988.

Haley, Alex and David Stevens. *Queen.* New York: William Morrow and Company, Inc., 1993.

Haley, Alex. *Roots.* New York: Doubleday, 1976.

Lester, Julius. *To Be A Slave.* New York: Dell-Yearling Books, 1968.

Myers, Walter Dean. *Malcolm X, By Any Means Necessary.* New York: Scholastic, Inc., 1993.

Myers, Walter Dean. *Now is Your Time.* New York: Harper Collins, 1991.

Index

University of Tennessee, 106, 109, 111–112, 114

Haley, Bertha Palmer, 12, 14–16, 18, 21–22, 53, 94–95

Haley, George, 20, 41, 93, 104, 109–111

Haley House Museum, 94–95

Haley, Julius, 21, 27

Haley, Lois, 21

Haley, Queen, 21, 99–101, 112

Haley, Simon, 12–14, 16, 18, 20–23, 25, 27–29, 52, 70, 99

Haley, Zeona Hatcher, 21, 27

Hamilton College, 59, 64, 66, 87

Henning, Tenn., 6, 14, 16, 18, 21, 23, 52, 62, 91, 103, 108

Home to Henning, 91, 98, 110

J

Jamaica, 71

K

King, Martin Luther, 42, 45, 54, 78

Kinte/Kin-tay, 6, 8, 54, 60, 62, 65, 70–71, 75, 79–80, 83, 86, 93

Knoxville, Tenn., 96, 111

L

Lear, Norman, 91–92

Lewis, Myran, 96

Los Angeles, Calif., 8–9, 74, 90, 96

M

Malcolm X, 40, 42–49, 51–54, 66, 103, 107, 111

Manga, Ebou, 60–62

Montgomery, Fred, 25, 95, 108

Muhammad, Elijah, 40, 44, 47

Muslims, 40–41, 45, 47

N

Nation of Islam, 40, 42, 44, 45, 47

P

Palmer, Cynthia Murray, 16, 18, 52–55, 59, 94

Palmer, Will, 16, 18–20, 25, 94

"Palmerstown, USA," 91–92

Playboy, 42–43, 45, 50

Pulitzer Prize, 9, 11, 78, 109

Q

Queen,
  book, 99, 110
  miniseries, 111–112

R

race relations, 29, 39, 41–42, 47–48, 53, 56, 74, 77, 79, 91, 101, 103, 110

Reader's Digest, 7–8, 40, 41, 57, 68, 69, 72

Rome, N.Y., 46

Roots: The Saga of An American Family, 8–11, 72–73, 74–75, 78–79, 81–86, 89–91, 93, 104, 108–110, 112–114, 116

Roots, the miniseries, 75–78, 80, 96–97

Roots: The Next Generation/ Roots II, 91

S

San Francisco, Calif., 36, 38, 39

segregation, 20–21, 36–37, 41–42, 56, 99, 103

Sims, George, 25, 38, 46, 57, 63, 66, 96, 98

slavery, 6–7, 40–41, 42, 53–54, 57, 59–60, 62, 64, 66–68, 75, 78–79, 83–84, 90, 93, 98–99, 108, 112, 114

Spingarn Medal, 78, 109